of the
Savior

Published Volumes

Revelation of the Unknowable God, Karen L. King

Gospel of the Savior, Charles W. Hedrick and Paul A. Mirecki

Gospel of the *Savior*

A New Ancient Gospel

Charles W. Hedrick
Paul A. Mirecki

Photographs used by permission of Ägyptisches Museum.

Polebridge Press is the publishing arm of the Westar Institute, a non-profit, public-benefit research and educational organization. To learn more, visit westarinstitute.org.

Library of Congress Cataloging-in-Publication Data
Gospel of the Savior : a new ancient Gospel / [edited] by Charles W. Hedrick, Paul A. Mirecki.
      p. cm. -- (California classical library)
   Includes bibliographical references and indexes.
   ISBN 978-0-944344-90-3
   1. Jesus Christ--Words. I. Hedrick, Charles W. II. Mirecki, Paul Allan. III. Series.
BS2860.Z8G67 1999
229′ .8--dc21   99-19383
                                                  CIP

10 9 8 7 6 5 4 3 2

Contents

Preface

As with any new manuscript discovery, determining its historical value and significance begins with a carefully presented edition of its text, which allows a thorough review by scholars in the field. This book is the beginning of that process. It includes a critical introduction and commentary, a transcription and translation of the Coptic text with notes, an index of Coptic words, and photographic reproductions of the parchment fragments. The book will serve as an introduction to this new discovery for those who are not expert in this area, as well as for the Scholar.

This has been a collaborative work, but primary responsibility for the transcription and translation has been assumed by Charles W. Hedrick. Paul A. Mirecki has assumed primary responsibility for the commentary and the indices. We have each critiqued the work of the other and together assume responsibility for the issues discussed in the introduction. The transcription and translation have been reviewed by Hans-Martin Schenke, Wolf-Peter Funk, and Douglas M. Parrott. In particular Schenke and Funk took considerable time from their own projects to engage issues relating to text and translation. It is fair to say that the transcription and translation have been significantly improved by their insightful critique and creative suggestions. April De Conick and Marvin W. Meyer have reviewed the commentary and made suggestions for improvement. Arthur J. Dewey and Daryl D. Schmidt have read the manuscript in its entirety and made suggestions for improvement. The authors are grateful to Wolf-Peter Funk for making available his unpublished computer generated concordance of Coptic and Greek forms of the Gospel of the Savior for use in the preparation of this volume. Edward F. Maniscalco has rendered invaluable assistance in seeing the volume through the editorial process and prepared the index of ancient texts and authors. Responsibility for the work, however, remains with the authors.

The critical text and translation have been presented on facing pages in diplomatic format. The goal for the critical translation was to produce a more literal, rather than a dynamically equivalent (and hence more interpretive) or colloquial translation. The goal for the commentary was to provide a scholarly discussion of critical issues for the specialist and non-specialist alike. The photographs from which the plates for this volume were made were prepared by Ms. Margarete Büsing, Photographer of the Egyptian Museum in Berlin. Financial support for Mirecki was provided by the National Endowment for the Humanities (summer stipend), the University of Kansas General Research Fund, and the Hall Center for the Humanities. Hedrick was supported by the National Endowment for the Humanities (summer stipend), and by a sabbatical leave from Southwest Missouri State University.

Where possible, references to text and translation use Coptic page and line numbers (or paragraph and sayings numbers). Leaves that have not been assigned a page number, since their arrangement in the codex is uncertain, are cited by their fragment number noted in the plates. Because the text was so fragmentary, we have preserved the process of its reconstruction by retaining the fragment number in the plates. The double columns presented a special difficulty. Usually in publication of texts having double columns on a page, the first column on a page is designated column A and the second column is column B, or column 1 and column 2. In the case of this text, there were three disconnected sheets of two leaves each, both having two columns, or vestiges of two columns. Initially we did not even know the direction of the fold of the sheets. In the reconstruction process the first two columns on the left-hand page of a sheet were designated A; on the right hand page they were designated B. We have retained this designation in the plates to preserve the process of reconstruction and hopefully to make it easier for scholars to verify our work. In cases where we had only one leaf from a sheet preserved, columns were designated column 1 and column 2, so as to distinguish the independent leaves from the sheets. Numbering the lines of both columns of a page seriatim made it unnecessary to cite the text by columns. Those who wish to work with the plates as opposed to the critical text should easily be able to orient themselves.

Kudos is due to Charlene Matejovsky and Geneviève Duboscq, and the staff of Polebridge Press, for the beauty of this volume's design and layout. To Charlene Matejovsky, Director of Polebridge Press, goes our deepest appreciation for her insistence on clarity in all phases of this book's production. Her patient and professional probing has made this volume more accessible to the specialist, and particularly to the general reader.

Conclusions presented in this book must be regarded as tentative. We felt it was more important to make a critical edition and an initial commentary of the text available to the public as soon as possible, rather than to aim at an exhaustive treatment and attempt to answer all questions and address all issues. This new gospel will find its proper position in the history of early Christian literature only with time, and after it has been intensely studied by many scholars.

To Our Teachers

Helmut Koester

James M. Robinson

Sigla

.   Sublinear dots beneath letters in the Coptic transcription indicate that the letters are not visually certain. Dots outside brackets in the transcription indicate vestiges of illegible Coptic letters. Each dot represents one letter. Dots appearing inside brackets in the transcription represent the number of Coptic letters it is calculated is missing in the lacuna. Each dot represents one letter. In cases where a ɴ is certain, but its expected supralinear stroke is not visible the entire letter is noted as uncertain by a sublinear dot (n̄). When iota is expected to appear with the diaersis but no part of the diaersis is visible, the entire letter is noted as uncertain (ï).

[ ]   Square brackets in the transcription indicate a lacuna in the manuscript where it is believed that writing once existed. Where the text cannot be reconstructed, the number of estimated letters in the lacuna up to four is indicated by sublinear dots; five or more missing letters are indicated by an Arabic number followed by a plus/minus (±) sign to indicate conjecture, since even the same Coptic letter elsewhere in the text can vary in size. When an unrestored lacuna occurs at the end of a line, the right margin is not closed with a bracket, since the number of Coptic letters in a line may vary. In the translation, words are not divided by brackets. A word is placed entirely in or out of brackets depending on the translator's judgment as to its certainty or uncertainty.

\ /   High diagonal strokes enclose letters that are written above the normal line of Coptic text.

( )   Parentheses in the translation indicate material supplied by the translator for the sake of clarity, or enclose the Greek form of loan words used in the Coptic text. Parentheses in the transcription enclose the line-final ɴ, when it is written as a supralinear stroke.

⟦ ⟧   Double square brackets indicate a scribal deletion.

*   An asterisk used with a page number indicates that the actual Coptic page number is unknown. The number has been assigned to the page to simplify its citation. This was necessary with fragment 4.

< >   Pointed brackets indicate an editorial correction by the modern editor of an ancient scribal error. A note records the actual reading of the manuscript.

Abbreviations

AcJohn	Acts of John	f.	feminine noun
AcPet12Apos	Acts of Peter and the	Gal	Galatians
	Twelve Apostles	GEgypt	Gospel of the
AcThom	Acts of Thomas		Egyptians
Acts	Acts	Gen	Genesis
adj.	adjective	Gk	Greek
adv.	adverb	GkAcThom	Greek Acts of
ApJas	Apocryphon of		Thomas
	James	GkApocPaul	Greek Apocalypse of
ApJohn	Apocryphon of John		Paul
ApocAb	Apocalypse of	GkApocPet	Greek Apocalypse of
	Abraham		Peter
ApocAdam	Apocalypse of Adam	GMary	Gospel of Mary
1-2 ApocJas	Apocalypse of James	GNaz	Gospel of the
ApocPaul	Apocalypse of Paul		Nazoreans
ApocPet	Apocalypse of Peter	GNic	Gospel of
ApocThom	Apocalypse of		Nicodemus
	Thomas	GPet	Gospel of Peter
ApocZeph	Apocalypse of	GPhil	Gospel of Philip
	Zephaniah	GSav	Gospel of the Savior
AscenIs	Ascension of Isaiah	GThom	Gospel of Thomas
Asclepius	Asclepius	GTruth	Gospel of Truth
AuthTeach	Authoritative	Heb	Hebrews
	Teaching	HypArch	Hypostasis of the
Clem	Clement		Archons
Col	Colossians	Ign	Ignatius
Copt	Coptic	IgnRom	Romans
1-2 Cor	1-2 Corinthians	IgnSm	Smyrnaeans
Dan	Daniel	IgnPol	Polycarp
Deut	Deuteronomy	IgnPhd	Philadelphians
Did	Teaching of the	IgnEph	Ephesians
	Twelve (Didache)	IgnTr	Trallians
DSav	Dialogue of the	IgnMag	Magnesians
	Savior	impv.	imperative verb
EgerG	Egerton Gospel	InterKnow	Interpretation of
EpApos	Epistula		Knowledge
	Apostolorum	intr.	intransitive verb
Eph	Ephesians	InJas	Infancy James
2 Esd	2 Esdras	InThom	Infancy Thomas
Eth	Ethiopic	Iren	Irenaeus
Exod	Exodus	AdvHaer	Adversus haereses
Ezek	Ezekiel	Isa	Isaiah
Ezra	Ezra	Jas	James

Jer	Jeremiah	SV	Scholars Version
Job	Job	TeachSilv	Teachings of
1-2-3 John	1-2-3 John		Silvanus
Jude	Jude	ThomCont	Book of Thomas the
Justin	Justin (Martyr)		Contender
Apol	Apology	1-2 Thess	1-2 Thessalonians
DialTrypho	Dialogue with	1-2 Tim	1-2 Timothy
	Trypho the Jew	TLevi	Testament of Levi
1-2 Kgs	1-2 Kings	tr.	transitive verb
Lev	Leviticus	TreatRes	Treatise on the
Luke	Gospel of Luke		Resurrection
LXX	Septuagint: Greek	TreatSeth	Second Treatise of
	translation of the		the Great Seth
	OT	TriTrac	Tripartite Tractate
m.	masculine noun	TTruth	Testimony of Truth
Mal	Malachi	WisSol	Wisdom of Solomon
Mark	Gospel of Mark	Zech	Zechariah
Matt	Gospel of Matthew	Zeph	Zephaniah
ms(s)	manuscript(s)	Zost	Zostrianos
n.	neuter (Greek) noun		
NHC	Nag Hammadi		
	Codices		
OdesSol	Odes of Solomon		
OnAnoint	On the Anointing		
OrWorld	On the Origin of the		
	World		
OT	Old Testament		
1-2 Pet	1-2 Peter		
Phil	Philippians		
pl.	plural		
POxy	Papyrus		
	Oxyrhynchus		
PG	J. Migne, *Patrologia*		
	Graeca		
Psa, Ps(s)	Psalm(s)		
qual.	qualitative verb		
Rev	Revelation		
Rom	Romans		
sg.	singular		
Sir	Sirach		
SMark	Secret Gospel of		
	Mark		
SophJesChr	Sophia of Jesus		
	Christ		

Introduction

The discovery of a new early Christian gospel, even though fragmentary, is an exciting surprise. While others have been discovered in the past, such discoveries are rare. Every new discovery, like the Gospel of the Savior, presents the possibility of new literary and historical data for current research into Christian origins. An early Christian "gospel" is a text comprised completely of sayings attributed to Jesus and/or brief stories about him, or a lengthy narrative about his public career containing both sayings and brief stories. A number of these non-canonical gospels, discovered and published in modern times,[1] arguably may date from the first or second-century common era.[2] Many of the earliest have only been discovered and published since the beginning of this century, and some even more recently.[3]

Scholars also know of other gospels written during the early period that are now lost. Fragments of some of them, however, survive only in the writings of the early leaders of the church, who quoted excerpts from them largely for the purposes of refutation.[4] Others survive as sources incorporated into the gospels of later writers.[5] Scholars are aware of such discoveries, and use these texts in reconstructing the history of early Christianity. The public at large, however, is not generally familiar with them and is surprised to learn that there is much more information available about Jesus than one finds in the four canonical gospels. These other gospels are important because they provide the modern scholar with a broader context for understanding Christian origins, and document early ways of understanding Jesus that differed from the canonical gospels.

The Gospel of the Savior has new sayings of Jesus and offers new opportuni-

---

1. See Wilhelm Schneemelcher and R. McL. Wilson, eds., *New Testament Apocrypha: Volume One: Gospels and Related Writings*; Volume Two: *Writings Relating to the Apostles, Apocalypses and Related Subjects*, rev. ed. (Louisville: Westminster/John Knox Press, 1991, 1992).

2. See Robert. J. Miller, ed., *The Complete Gospels: Annotated Scholars Version*, rev. ed. (Sonoma, Calif.: Polebridge Press, 1994).

3. Schneemelcher and Wilson, *New Testament Apocrypha*, Vol. 1, and Miller, *Complete Gospels*. The Gospel of Thomas, discovered in 1945 and published in 1952 (the Greek fragments were discovered earlier near the turn of the century and were not then recognized as the Gospel of Thomas); the Dialogue of the Savior, discovered in 1945 and published in 1984 (English translation in 1977); the Secret Gospel of Mark, discovered in 1958 and published in 1973; Egerton Papyrus 2, discovered in 1934 and published in 1935 (a second fragment was discovered in 1987); Papyrus Oxyrhynchus 840, discovered in 1905, and published in 1908; Papyrus Oxyrhynchus 1224, discovered in 1903 and published in 1914; the Gospel of Mary, fragments published in 1938, 1955, and 1983.

4. See Miller, *Complete Gospels*, 425–46. These are the gospels of the Nazoreans, the Hebrews, and the Ebionites.

5. The sayings gospel Q and the Signs Gospel: See Miller, *Complete Gospels*, 249–300; 175–95.

1

ties for evaluating sayings already known from the canonical gospels and the Gospel of Thomas. The Gospel of the Savior is a remnant at one time consisting of approximately 30 pages from a larger work. The original length of the document remains unknown. The extant fragments consist of a dialogue between the savior and the apostles shortly before the crucifixion, and feature visionary ascents by the Savior and the apostles into the heavens, similar to the ascent into the third heaven alluded to by Paul in 2 Cor 12:1–10. In one soliloquy the savior also courageously addresses the cross that he soon will "mount," a very different image from the irresolute Jesus of Mark's gospel, who is "greatly distressed and troubled" as he faced the cross (Mark 14:33–34). The latest date for its original composition is probably in the late second century.

Every new manuscript discovery, however, must be carefully analyzed to determine its significance for understanding the past. The process to determine its historical value begins with a careful edition and analysis of its text, which allow thorough review by scholars in the field. This book is the beginning of that process for a previously unknown, but ancient, early Christian gospel.

Acquisition, Discovery, and Conservation

The Gospel of the Savior (Papyrus Berolinensis 22220) is a collection of parchment fragments that were acquired by the Berlin Egyptian Museum (Charlottenburg) from the Dutch antiquities dealer Karl J. Möger on March 20, 1967, for 300 Deutsch Marks.6 The card catalogue of the museum confirms the 1967 date. A note, handwritten in ink and included with the fragments, reads as follows:

> 22220 Fragmente mehrere Pergamum Blätter: neutestamentlicher Apokryphon (angebliche Reden Jesu). Etwa 6 Jh. (alt!). Vorsicht!

> 22220 several fragmentary parchment leaves: new Testament Apocryphon (apparently discourses of Jesus). Circa 6th century (old!). Caution!

It is unknown who wrote the note or when it was placed there, but apparently, shortly after the acquisition of the fragments, someone read enough of them to realize that they contained speeches of Jesus. The geographical region from which the text originated is unknown.

In 1991, at the suggestion of William Brashear, the museum's curator of manuscripts, Paul A. Mirecki selected approximately 120 unstudied (and not yet conserved) fragmentary Coptic manuscripts from the metal storage boxes in the

---

6. A handwritten note with the fragments indicates that they were purchased in 1971 ("Ankauf März '71"). According to the museum acquisitions book for the years 1969–1976, however, no parchment fragments were listed as being purchased in 1971.

archives of the museum plus 28 others (inventory numbers of these 28 were 22196–22223) that had been conserved since the 1969 publication of volume three of Coptic Manuscripts in the Berlin Egyptian Museum.[7] Mirecki is preparing to publish a new collection of Coptic texts from the Berlin collection. He spent the summers of 1991 and 1993 cleaning, restoring, and editing these texts and, at the same time, made transcriptions of the two largest fragments of P22220, the Gospel of the Savior. He also made photographs of some of the texts he was studying to use in the United States, including life size photocopies of the Gospel of the Savior. At that time, Mirecki considered the fragments to be extracts from a Coptic homily having paraphrasing from the gospels. Since further study of the fragments was unrelated to his then current project of cataloguing unstudied manuscripts, he set them aside for later study.

During the summers of 1991 and 1993 the fragments of the Gospel of the Savior were seen by Mirecki stored in four large paper folders in one of the cupboards in the archive area. The largest fragment, temporarily placed between unsealed glass, rested on the light table in the archive area, where Brashear first showed it to Mirecki in 1991, and where Hedrick also saw it in 1995.

In January 1995 the fragments of the Gospel of the Savior had not yet been permanently conserved, but were still temporarily placed in four large paper folders and one unsealed glass plate. An initial counting and preliminary numbering system for the folders and glass plate and their contents were completed in January 1995 by Hedrick.[8] The contents were:

Folder one: a fragmentary leaf (= two pages) inscribed on both sides, having vestiges of two columns on each side, and eleven smaller fragments inscribed on both sides.

Folder two: two fragments, one of which was a fragmentary leaf (= two pages), having two columns of text on each page.

Folder three: one fragmentary sheet (= two leaves = four pages), inscribed on both sides with vestiges of two columns of text on each page.

Folder four: a fragmentary sheet (= two leaves = four pages) inscribed on both sides. One of the leaves contained vestiges of two columns on both sides. Folder four also contained thirteen other smaller fragments inscribed on both sides.

The unsealed glass plate: four small fragments inscribed on both sides, and a fragmentary sheet (= two leaves = four pages) inscribed on both sides with two columns of text on each page.

---

7. Helmut Satzinger, ed., *Koptische Urkunden* (Ägyptische Urkunden aus der Staatlichen Museen Berlin 3; Berlin: Bruno Hessling, 1968).

8. See the preliminary report on the fragments presented at the sixth meeting of the International Association of Coptic Studies Münster, Germany 20–26 July 1996: Charles W. Hedrick, "A Preliminary Report on Coptic Codex P. Berol. Inv. 22220," to appear in *Akten des 6. Internationalen Koptologenkrongresses.*

Thus, there were three fragmentary sheets, two fragmentary leaves, and twenty-nine smaller fragments that comprised the Gospel of the Savior—a total of thirty-four fragments in all. This was exactly the same condition of the fragments when seen by Mirecki in 1991, based on a comparison with the life size photocopies made by him at that time. In March of 1995 Hedrick made photographs of the fragments in that state of conservation, which he later used to critique the transcription of the fragments prepared from the parchment during the work session at the museum January through March 1995.

During work sessions in the museum June and July 1996, and December 1996 through January 1997, Hedrick assembled some of the fragments and arranged them all in eight glass plates.[9] Each fragment has now been assigned an individual number in the collection, rather than in relation to the glass plates in which they have been conserved. This was done in order to simplify the accounting system, and thus to make description of the text more precise for its initial study, and for subsequent study. As a result of fragments placed during these two work sessions and later, there are now a total of twenty-eight fragments in the eight plates that comprise the Gospel of the Savior. The collection was put in a final state of conservation in the spring of 1997 by the museum conservator, Mr. Jürgen Hofman, Papyrus Restorer. The photographs for this volume were prepared in March 1997 by the Museum Photographer, Ms. Margarete Büsing.

Codicological Analysis

The original dimensions of the leaves of the codex from which these fragments came can only be estimated from measurements of the largest fragmentary sheet (frg. 1). The leaves of this sheet at its widest points are 19.6 cm in breadth and 24.9 cm in height (see the plates). Hence the page dimensions of the original codex appear to be closest to Turner's group V of parchment codices (17–20 cm in breadth, and 21–25 cm in height).[10] The margins around the text at its widest points are as follows: 2.4 cm at the top; 4.4 cm at the bottom; 2.0 cm from the center fold to the beginning of the left hand margin of text; approximately 2.0 cm from the end of the right margin of text to the right hand edge of the page, and 1.0–1.8 cm between the two columns of a page.

The attempt to uncover some connection among the fragments was made more difficult by the sheets. Each sheet had four columns, or vestiges of four

9. Later, in 1997, working only with the text supplied by Hedrick, Wolf-Peter Funk identified the location of fragment eight at the top of both columns of 4F/H on the basis of a continuation of text between columns on each page.

10. Eric G. Turner, *The Typology of the Early Codex* (Philadelphia: University of Pennsylvania Press, 1977).

columns, to its hair side and four to its skin side. It was clear that the text from the bottom of the second column on the left hand half of the sheets was not continued by the text on the top of the first column of the right hand half of the sheets, as it would have to do, if one sheet had been folded inside another to form part of the same quire. Thus, with regard to the sheets, there were two pages on each side of a single sheet that at one time were separated by another sheet, or sheets, when the quires were bound in the codex. To keep the pages distinguished, the two columns of the left hand page of an open sheet were designated A columns and those on the right hand page were designated B columns (hence the A and B designations in the plates). Initially, we distinguished between the columns as column 1 and column 2, but once we decided to number the lines on a page seriatim we could dispense with distinguishing between columns.[11]

The entire collection of fragments appears to represent at least 30 pages. With so few fragments extant, however, their relationship to one another and their position in the codex from which they were extracted would appear to be impossible to determine. Certain information, however, helps to identify aspects of the original codex configuration of some of the fragments. All three of the sheets (frgs. 1, 2, and 4) fold with the hair side (H) of the sheet inside the fold, and the flesh side (F) outside the fold. This observation establishes the arrangement of these sheets in the codex configuration but not their sequence. One of the sheets fortunately had page numbers on one of its leaves: frg. 2F/H (= pages 99/100). In 1996 another page number was identified among the smaller fragments and placed on frg. 1. The placement was possible because the text had previously been restored on the basis of a parallel between the Gospel of the Savior and the Gospel of John. Thus 1F/H became pages 107/108. The restored text of page 107.31–36 is as follows: "But indeed do not touch me, until I go/ up to [my Father] who [is] your [Father] and [my God who] is your God" (cf. John 20:17). This restoration confirmed the placement of the fragment having the page numbers, and thereby established the exact sequence of frg. 2 and 1 in relationship to one another and in the original codex from which they were taken.

On the basis of a fortunate continuation of text between frgs. 3F and 2F (= page 99), these two parchment pages had to be facing one another in the original codex configuration. Fragment 3F.63–2F.3 reads as follows:

"For it is written that I will strike [the shepherd] and/ [they] will be scattered, namely the sheep of the flock" (cf. Zech 13:7 and Matt 26:31).

---

11. Chassinat also used a seriatim numbering for lines of a double column codex; see M.É.Chassinat, *Le quatrième livre des entretiens et épitres de Shenouti* (Mémoires publiés par les membres de l'institut français d'archéologie orientale 23; Cairo: Imprimerie de l'institut français d'archéologie orientale, 1911). This parallel was brought to our attention by Wolf-Peter Funk.

Thus frg. 3F is Coptic page [98] because it immediately precedes Coptic page 99, and 3H therefore must be Coptic page [97]. The relationship of frg. 3H/F contiguous to 2F/H is also evidence that the codex from which this text was extracted follows the usual rotation of sheets in parchment codices, alternating them so that hair side faces hair side and flesh side faces flesh side.[12]

Thus there are three page numbers among the fragments, pages [97]/[98] (=frg. 3H/F), pages 99/100 (=frg.2F/H), and pages 107/108 (=frg.1F/H), establishing the size of the gathering of sheets to which frg. 2 belonged (see fig. 1). Fragments 3 and 1 therefore must belong to adjacent gatherings of sheets. Figure 1 projects that these two adjacent gatherings (quires 1 and 3) consisted of at least two sheets each. Actually early parchment codices were never that regular in the number of sheets contained in gatherings, and hence gathering 1 and 3 in figure 1 may have consisted of more sheets, but it is unlikely that they had less than two sheets.[13]

We have not been successful in connecting the remaining two larger fragments (frgs. 4 and 5) to the sequential arrangement of frgs. 3, 2, 1 (depicted in figure 1). On the basis of similar content, however, it is quite possible that frg. 5 may have been the bottom to frg. 2. Fragment 2H (B) = p. [105] has an unknown figure addressing a singular "you" (ⲚⲦⲔ line 40), and twice in this column the cross is mentioned (lines 42, 47). The reverse side of this leaf, 2F(A)= p. 106 (see figure 1), has an address to an unspecified singular "you" (ⲤⲎⲦⲔ, line 40) and also an address to the cross (lines 44–47). The only other location among the larger fragments where this combination (singular "you" addressed, and the noun "cross") appears is on frg. 5, where there are a series of sayings to the cross addressed as "you." On p. [114].64 the antecedent of the singular "you" is unclear. Among the smaller fragments the word "cross" appears (mostly in lacuna) in 7F.3/7H.36; 11H.30. The cross is addressed (mostly in lacuna) in 122*.35; and in 11F.30. The singular "you" with unclear antecedents also appears in 10F.4; 11H.32 (possibly); 17H.2 (possibly); 21F.3/21H.3 (possibly); 23F.1.

Based on these observations, a connection can possibly be made between frg. 2 as the top of the leaf and frg. 5 as its bottom as follows: on frg. 5H the first extant line in col. 2 (=line 51) becomes line 51 of p. [105]. Thus one must project one line lost in lacuna following p. [105].49 and line 51 of frg. 5H. Page [106] and frg. 5F would make connection as follows: the first extant line of frg. 5F, would become line 19 of p. [106]. Thus one line (line 18) is lacking between p. [106].17 and frg. 5F.19.

12. See Turner, *Typology of the Early Codex*, 56.
13. See Turner, *Typology of the Early Codex*, 61–64. Turner knows of no parchment codices comprised completely of two sheets to each gathering, or one sheet to each gathering. Codices having generally two sheets per gathering are mixed and include gatherings of three and four sheets interspersed among the two sheet gatherings. Thus certainty about the number of sheets in gatherings 1 and 3 in figure 1 is not possible.

Possibly frg. 4F(B) follows immediately after p. [114] in the codex and thus begins a new quire as p. [115], but that is uncertain. We have numbered frg. 4 in the page sequence of frgs. 1–3 merely for convenience in citation. To indicate its uncertain placement we have marked it with an asterisk (see the plates and the text/translation). The extant text of 4F(B).29–31 describes the "son" doing something (coming? saying?) "for the third time." This statement taken in connection with p. [114].62–63, where a reference to "[the] second time" is found, suggests a continuation of the scene appearing on p. [114]. The statement on p. [114].62–63 may not be a reference to the Gethsemane prayer of Jesus, however, since p. [114].6–9, 24–27 also portray the "son" praying, apparently in Gethsemane. Note also a reference to "[the] second" on p. 106.15–16. Fragment 4F/H is printed here immediately following 1H/F rather than frg. 5F/H because 4F/H constitutes the vestiges of a complete sheet while 5F/H constitutes the remains of a leaf.

There are three smaller fragments having a virtually identical shape: frgs. 19, 20, 21. They are arranged in the glass plates in the Berlin museum according to their shape, not on the basis of hair side/flesh side. In reality, frg. 19 hair side and frg. 20 hair side appear in the glass plate labeled flesh side. They are correctly identified in this volume. Thus because of their identical shape, the sequence of frgs. 19, 20, 21 were most probably adjacent to one another in the codex, or in these remnants of the Gospel of the Savior before deterioration. They would have appeared in one of the following two series: 19H/F, 21F/H, 20H/F or 20H/F, 21F/H, 19H/F.[14] There is no way to be certain which series represents the actual codex configuration.

The judgment that these three fragments appeared as a part of adjacent leaves in the codex configuration or in the extract of sheets that constitute the Gospel of the Savior is based on their nearly identical pattern of deterioration. Since it has not been possible to place these three fragments with any of the larger fragmentary sheets and leaves, they likely represent missing leaves from quire 1 (figure 1), missing leaves from quire 3 (assuming it to have been comprised of more than two sheets), or the remains of three additional leaves of yet a fourth quire.

In summary, the entire collection of extant fragments represents a minimum of eight leaves or sixteen pages of a work that was originally larger. Because of the extant page numbers and a fortuitous continuation of text between one leaf and one of the sheets, there is a sequence of text among six of the leaves as follows: [97], [98], 99, 100, (101–104 lost), [105], [106], 107, 108, (109–112 lost), [113], [114]. We have been unable to connect the last two larger fragments to the pre-

---

14. While the hair side/flesh side of the fragments could have been reversed, the sequence of the fragments would remain the same with frg. 21 as the middle fragment between 19 and 20. Fragment 22 is also very similar to the same shape of the series 19, 20, 21 and for that reason has been conserved on the basis of shape, not hair or flesh side.

Figure 1: *Paginating the Fragments*

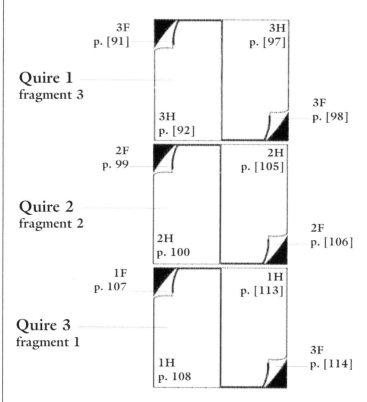

Quire 1
fragment 3

3F p. [91]	3H p. [97]
3H p. [92]	3F p. [98]

Quire 2
fragment 2

2F p. 99	2H p. [105]
2H p. 100	2F p. [106]

Quire 3
fragment 1

1F p. 107	1H p. [113]
1H p. 108	3F p. [114]

- Coptic page numbers 99 and 100 are clearly visible on frg. 2.
- The sentence that ends at the top of p. 99 begins at the end of frg. 3, consequently the last page of frg. 3 must be page number 98.
- Coptic page numbers 107 and 108 are clearly visible on frg. 1.
- Since 1F/H is numbered 107/108, there can only be two numbered sheets (=eight pages) in Quire two, and thus 2H/F must be pages 105/106.
- Based on the evidence provided by quire 2, this reconstruction projects each quire to be a gathering of 2 sheets (= 8 pages), though there could be more in quires 1 and 3. Thus quire 1 is projected to begin on (now lost) p. 91 (since p. 98 is the last page in the quire) and quire 3 to end on p. 114 (since quire 3 begins with p. 107).
- Consequently we are able to project page numbers for the extant material in the three quires as follows:

Quire 1 (frg. 3)   Pp. [97–98] (pp. 91–96 are lost)
Quire 2 (frg. 2)   Pp. 99–100, [105–106] (pp. 101–104 are lost)
Quire 3 (frg. 1)   Pp. 107–108, [113–114] (pp. 109–112 are lost)

ceding series with absolute certainty. Three smaller fragments having an identical shape must be construed as another six pages. So, if our reconstruction of the quires is correct, this vestige of an early Christian gospel at one time in antiquity consisted of 15 leaves or 30 pages at a minimum: eight extant leaves; plus two leaves lost between pages [100] and [105]; plus an additional two leaves lost between pages 108 and 113; plus 3 leaves represented by the identically shaped fragments. Since we have neither the beginning nor the ending of the text we have to conclude that it was originally larger than thirty pages.

Scribal Practice

The manufacturer, or the scribe, carefully prepared the parchment sheets for the writing of the text. Horizontal and vertical lines are scored into the leather on the hair side (the scoring on the hair side is deep enough to be used as a guide for writing on the skin side). Vertical lines delimit the width of columns, the empty space allowed between columns, and, as a result, the amount of space on the page to be inscribed. The scored horizontal lines serve as guides for the scribe's written lines, with one line of text for each scored line. The line-scoring to guide the text is clearly visible on frg. 1 between the columns on each leaf, and also on frgs. 5H, 2H, and 4H.

Fragment 1, the only nearly complete sheet in the collection, preserves both first and last lines on each leaf of the sheet. On all four pages of the sheet there are 32 lines per page. Hence, because of the scoring, and the scribe's consistency on the only nearly complete sheet in the collection, each leaf in the collection of fragments has been assumed to have 32 lines to each page. The number of letters per complete line of extant text varies from 10–13 letters with 11–12 being the usual number.

The Coptic hand is quite regular, and may even be described as elegant. There are a few scribal peculiarities. When certain letters are in the first or last line of a page, the scribe tends to decorate them, or otherwise emphasize them. When ⲣ is in the top line of a page, the scribe draws a coil into the margin from the top of the letter (2F, col.4; 1F, col. 4; 1H, col. 1; 7F; 4F, col. 2; but does not follow this practice for every ⲣ written in the first line: 2H, col. 2.

The scribe extends the tails of ⲱ, ⲩ, ⲣ, ⲧ, and ⲩ into the bottom margin when they appear in the last line of a page, sometimes with a coil on the letter ⲱ:

ⲣ: 1H; 5H; 4H, col. 1; but ⲣ is not always extended: 1F, col. 2; 1H, col. 2; 3F

ⲩ: 1H, col. 1; 4H, col. 2; but ⲩ is not always extended: 3H, col. 2; 4F, col. 2; 5H, col. 1; 11F

ⲱ: 5H; 4H; 1F; 13H; but ⲱ is not always decorated: 3F; 1H
ϥ: 11F; but ϥ is not always extended: 4H, col. 2
ϯ: 1F, col. 2; but ϯ is not always extended: 1F, col. 3

Occasionally at the ends of lines the letters ϥ, ⲣ, ⲩ, ⲧ and ϯ, are written above the regular line of text with the tail of the letter squeezed in between its two adjacent letters written on the regular line; the squeezed-in tail of the letter marks its orthographical location:

ⲣ: 4F, col. 1, line 1
ⲧ: 4H, col. 3, line 3
ⲩ: 10F, col. 1
ϥ: 1F, col. 3, line 4; 10H
ϯ: 5F, line 21; 1H, col. 2, line 4; 2H, col. 2, lines 10, 18, 20; 2F, col.
      2, line 8; 2F, col. 3, line 6; 9H

In the interests of saving space, the scribe will squeeze one letter written smaller than usual beneath another regular sized letter:

ⲉ: 2H, col. 3, line 9
ⲟ: 4F, col. 1, line 1; 17F; 2F, col. 3, line 1; 1F, col.1, line 9; 1H, col.
      1, line 1; 1H, col. 3, line 3; 4F, col. 2, line 28

Occasionally the scribe will abbreviate ⲛ as a supralinear stroke at the end of the line in order to save space: 2H, col. 2, line 17; 1F, col. 1, line 12; 1F, col. 3, line 12; 1H, col. 2, lines 26, 32; 1H, col. 3, line 8; 4H, col. 2, line 31, or will simply write a letter above the line (3H, col. 1, line 29: ⲟ).

When they come first in a line of text, certain letters are written oversized and extended into the left margin in order to mark the beginning of a specific saying (see also below):

ⲁ: 4F, col. 3, line 29; 1F, col. 3, line 24; 1H, col. 1, line 17
ⲉ: 1H, col. 2, line 14
ⲟ: 1H, col. 2, lines 2, 4
ⲡ: 1H, col. 1, line 19; 1H, col. 2, line 11
ⲥ: 1H, col. 2, line 27
ⲭ: 1F, col. 3, line 5; 2H, col. 3, lines 12, 16
ϯ: 1F, col. 4, line 17; 2H. col. 3, lines 5, 8

When written oversized and extended into the left margin ⲭ is decorated with coils on both its ears.

At 2F, col. 3, line 16 the scribe writes ⲡⲁ of ⲡⲁⲓⲱⲧ in the margin as regular sized letters, and not smaller, as one would expect if the letters had initially been omitted by scribal error; this also appears to be the case with ⲉ at 2H, col. 2, line 1.

The scribe uses two different devices to identify the beginnings of certain sayings in the text. One of these appears only once among the fragments at 1H col. 2, line 13 while the other appears in three different forms (figure 2).

Figure 2

In this text these devices appear to mark a major break in the sayings of the savior. The scribe begins the device at the beginning of the line to be emphasized and extends downward into the margin. The first letter of the line is written slightly larger than other letters in the line and is extended into the left margin. Hence these devices were likely employed at the time the current manuscript was copied and not later by a second or different scribe. Usually the preceding saying concludes with "Amen" and/or a dicolon to mark the major break. They appear at the following locations in the text:

3F, col. 2, line 15; 2F, col. 3, line 25; 2H, col. 3, lines 5, 8, 12, 16; 2H, col. 4, line 28; 1F, col. 3, lines 5, 10, 24; 1F, col. 4, lines 17, 26; 1H, col. 1, lines 17, 19; 1H, col. 2, lines 2, 4, 11, 14, 18, 27; 1H, col. 3, line 3; 4F, col. 3, line 23; 5H, col. 2, line 26.

Decorations also appear on the following fragments: 10F/H, 8F, 9F. There is no colored ink used in the extant fragments of the Gospel of the Savior.

There are few evident orthographical errors. ⲀⲨⲦⲞⲊⲞⲨⲤⲒⲞⲤ (p. 98.32) may be a scribal error for the usual ⲀⲨⲦⲈⲊⲞⲨⲤⲒⲞⲤ (αὐτεξούσιος). Apparently the scribe conceived of the word as αὐτός ἐξούσιος, i.e., as dropping the last letter of αὐτός and the first letter of ἐξούσιος, rather than the last two letters of αὐτός.

In another instance, the scribe has erased ⲟ and written ⲩ over the erased ⲟ (p. 100.1). Apparently the scribe intended to write ⲞⲨⲚⲀⲨ, but mistakenly wrote ⲞⲨⲚⲞ (for ⲞⲨⲚⲞⲨ), caught the error at the second ⲟ, erased it, but then mistakenly corrected ⲟ to ⲩ rather than to ⲁ, and then wrote ⲁ above the line to complete ⲞⲨⲚⲀⲨ. The scribe has apparently erroneously written ⲠⲨⲄⲎ (πυγή, rump) for ⲠⲎⲄⲎ (πηγή spring) at frg. 19H.5.

The scribe regularly abbreviates Greek σταυρός as ⲤⲢⲞⲤ and Jerusalem is once abbreviated as ⲐⲒⲀⲎⲙ (14F.27). Israel is twice abbreviated as ⲒⲎⲀ at p. 114.6, 13. Punctuation used by the scribe includes a point at the end of a unit of thought. It appears in both a high (ⲉ·) and low (ⲉ.) position. A dicolon (:) appears at major breaks, sometimes followed by a horizontal dash. An apostrophe occasionally appears at the end of the following letters: ⲁ', ⲕ', ⲗ', ⲙ', ⲛ', ⲥ'. A "comma" is found once following the word ⲕⲟⲥⲙⲟⲥ,: frg. 21H.2. Line-final ⲛ is frequently written as a supralinear stroke at the ends of lines. These instances are indicated in the text as follows: (ⲛ).

Language

The text is written in Sahidic Coptic, the dialect of Upper Egypt. With one possible exception, the language is standardized Sahidic, suggesting that this copy of the Gospel of the Savior dates after the fourth century C.E., at which time Sahidic had achieved standardization in orthography. There is one form some may regard as a dialectal variant. At p. 113.9–10 the scribe writes ⲡⲏⲟ[ⲩⲉ rather than ⲡⲏⲩⲉ (p. 113.1; p. 100.40, 51). Crum lists ⲡⲏⲟⲩⲉ as an Achmimic form and Kasser regards it as an archaic Sahidic form.[15] Wolf-Peter Funk regards it as a variant spelling (not a dialect form), which, he says, "is occasionally used even in the most classical of standard Sahidic manuscripts, especially when a line break appears to be necessary after ⲏ (and the new line can, of course, not be started with a naked ⲩ), or by inadvertent copying from a manuscript in which this happened to be the case." In another instance (p. 113.25), the scribe uses the nonstandard Sahidic spelling ⲁⲣⲭⲏⲁⲅⲅⲉⲗⲟⲥ (instead of the expected ⲁⲣⲭⲓⲁⲅⲅⲉⲗⲟⲥ), which is regularly found in later Fayyumic and Boharic texts.[16]

An unusual use of ϣⲟⲣⲡ⸗ suggests that the Gospel of the Savior is likely a translation of a Greek original. The Coptic ϣⲱⲣⲡ (Crum 586b) usually relates to time and has the temporal significance "to be early." It is regularly used in the reflexive with this temporal meaning. On p. 106.44–47 the reflexive is used as follows:

ⲕ/[ϣ]ⲟⲣⲡⲕ ⲉⲣⲟⲓ ⲱ̄ [ⲡ]ⲉ/ⲥⲡⲟⲥ
ⲁⲛⲟⲕ ϩ[ⲱⲱⲧ] ϯⲛⲁϣⲟⲣⲡⲧ ⲉⲣⲟⲕ

The usual use of the construction "to be early to/for" does not seem appropriate: "you are early to/for me, O cross; I also will be early to/for you." The Coptic ϣⲱⲣⲡ is used to translate the Greek ὀρθρίζειν.[17] Liddell and Scott list a

---

15. Rodolphe Kasser, *Compléments au dictionaire copte de Crum* (Cairo: l' institut français d'archéologie orientale, 1964), xii–xiii, 43.

16. According to Wolf-Peter Funk in private correspondence.

17. W.E. Crum, *A Coptic Dictionary* (Oxford: Clarendon, 1939), 586b.

Scribal Note

There is a scribal note written in a very poor documentary hand across the bottom margin of p. 97 upside down to the Coptic text on the page. Because frg. 3 is badly damaged from burning and, as a consequence, badly wrinkled and discolored on the hair side, the note is virtually illegible.

```
1.                                    ] . . [
2.                         ] . . [   a]ποστοлοι επ[ι
3.                 ] . . [   ]ογc ννα[   ] . κανο . αcτ[   ]πι
4.   [      ]μογ . [   ] . [   ]ετc . [   ]αι[
5.         ]εροι . . [   ]ω ωωϣ . . ρ . [   ]ρ . [
6.         ]ολ . . . το . παρα . . . . ιο . . [   ]μιc . . β . τ[
```

The only certain reading in this virtually illegible text is "apostles" (ἀπόστολοι) with a properly inflected plural ending in line 2. In line 5 ωωϣ may be an old Sahidic form of ωϣ "proclaim." The shift to Greek script in line 6 is surprising and suggests a two language environment for the note. The number of lines in the note is uncertain, as is the length of lines.

metaphorical use of ὀρθρίζειν that usually has the temporal idea of "being early" (cf. Luke 21:38), as carrying instead the idea of "be eager, or earnest" (cf. Jer 25:3, LXX) or "go eagerly, or earnestly" to/for (cf. Ps 62(63):1, LXX).[18] Recognizing ϣορπ̄ to be a literal translation of ὀρθρίζειν that misses its metaphorical use permits a translation of the Coptic as "I am eager for" or "I go eagerly to" in the Gospel of the Savior, and renders a reasonable sense to the text. This implies that the Gospel of the Savior is based on an earlier Greek original subsequently translated into Coptic.

Paleography and Date

The dating of this parchment manuscript must be based upon paleographic considerations, basically a comparison of its writing style with other datable Coptic manuscripts. The scribal hand is regular and quite elegant. There are no instances of deliberate ligation between letters. Except when crowding in letters at the ends of lines τ is written with two short dense down strokes to each end of the cross bar. The same strokes are also used with †, г, and ϥ.

18. H.G. Liddell and R. Scott, *A Greek-English Lexicon with a Supplement* (Oxford: Clarendon, 1968), supplement, 110.

Thus, there were three fragmentary sheets, two fragmentary leaves, and twenty-nine smaller fragments that comprised the Gospel of the Savior—a total of thirty-four fragments in all. This was exactly the same condition of the fragments when seen by Mirecki in 1991, based on a comparison with the life size photocopies made by him at that time. In March of 1995 Hedrick made photographs of the fragments in that state of conservation, which he later used to critique the transcription of the fragments prepared from the parchment during the work session at the museum January through March 1995.

During work sessions in the museum June and July 1996, and December 1996 through January 1997, Hedrick assembled some of the fragments and arranged them all in eight glass plates.[9] Each fragment has now been assigned an individual number in the collection, rather than in relation to the glass plates in which they have been conserved. This was done in order to simplify the accounting system, and thus to make description of the text more precise for its initial study, and for subsequent study. As a result of fragments placed during these two work sessions and later, there are now a total of twenty-eight fragments in the eight plates that comprise the Gospel of the Savior. The collection was put in a final state of conservation in the spring of 1997 by the museum conservator, Mr. Jürgen Hofman, Papyrus Restorer. The photographs for this volume were prepared in March 1997 by the Museum Photographer, Ms. Margarete Büsing.

Codicological Analysis

The original dimensions of the leaves of the codex from which these fragments came can only be estimated from measurements of the largest fragmentary sheet (frg. 1). The leaves of this sheet at its widest points are 19.6 cm in breadth and 24.9 cm in height (see the plates). Hence the page dimensions of the original codex appear to be closest to Turner's group V of parchment codices (17–20 cm in breadth, and 21–25 cm in height).[10] The margins around the text at its widest points are as follows: 2.4 cm at the top; 4.4 cm at the bottom; 2.0 cm from the center fold to the beginning of the left hand margin of text; approximately 2.0 cm from the end of the right margin of text to the right hand edge of the page, and 1.0–1.8 cm between the two columns of a page.

The attempt to uncover some connection among the fragments was made more difficult by the sheets. Each sheet had four columns, or vestiges of four

9. Later, in 1997, working only with the text supplied by Hedrick, Wolf-Peter Funk identified the location of fragment eight at the top of both columns of 4F/H on the basis of a continuation of text between columns on each page.

10. Eric G. Turner, *The Typology of the Early Codex* (Philadelphia: University of Pennsylvania Press, 1977).

All the fragments clearly belong to the same hand. Before their conservation, however, there was one small fragment from a different hand that was removed and conserved apart from the fragments that comprise the Gospel of the Savior.

Based on a comparison of the hand of the Gospel of the Savior with manuscripts that can be dated, the hand of this text has affinities with texts dating from the fourth to the seventh centuries C.E. Parchment manuscripts having two columns to a page are known as early as the second century C.E. and are common from the fourth century C.E.[19] On the basis of paleography, a date later than the seventh century seems unlikely, though one can scarcely be certain. These judgments were made using the examples in Maria Cramer[20] and comparing them to the following letters from the Gospel of the Savior: ⲁ, ⲉ, ⲑ, ⲗ, ⲙ, ⲟ, ⲡ, ⲧ, ⲩ, ϯ, 6, as well as considering the general appearance of the sample of text in which the letters were found. The numbers in columns below represent the sample number in Cramer.

	4th C	5th C	5–6th C	6–7th C
ⲁ		8	11 & 14	15
ⲉ	2c & 3	7	12 & 14	
ⲑ	2a & 2b			16
ⲗ	3			
ⲙ		7 & 8	14	15
ⲟ	4	7	14	16
ⲡ	3			
ⲧ		7	13	15 & 16
ⲩ	2a, c & 3		13 & 14	15
ϭ	1 & 2c		12 & 14	
ϯ			14	16
6				16

There can be little question that the larger fragments (1, 2, 3, 4, 5) reflect a content consistent with one another, and with the identification of the text as a "gospel."[21] This is also true of most of the smaller fragments (7, 8, 9, 10, 11,

---

19. Turner, *Typology of the Early Codex*, 101–85. Turner dates #47 as second century C.E.
20. *Koptische Paläographie* (Wiesbaden: Otto Harrassowitz, 1964).
21. A question can be raised about frg. 4H.63 because of the restoration ⲧⲁ]ⲓⲧⲟⲩⲣⲅⲓⲁ (= λειτουργία, meaning "public service" or perhaps "liturgy"). But compare Luke 1:23 where the word is used in a gospel text. The rest of the vocabulary on this sheet can be seen as consistent with that of the other fragments, however.

12, 14, 17, 20, 21, 22, 23, 25). There is not enough text extant on fragments 6, 13, 15, 16, 18, 26, 27 to allow a judgment as to the consistency of vocabulary with the larger fragments. The hand of these fragments is the same as the larger fragments, however. (Fragment 16 has no letters that can be read with certainty.) Two fragments, however, feature vocabulary that seems odd for a "gospel" text (frgs. 19 and 24). Fragment 24H in addition appears to have the character of a list (see the commentary), although 24F might be seen as fitting quite well with the rest of the fragments as part of a gospel text.

Contents and History of Religions Context

We have given the text from which these fragments come the modern title the Gospel of the Savior because the fragments suggest that it was comprised of brief collections of sayings set in a dialogue frame between the "savior" (p. 100.1, 50; p. 107.24, 54; p. 113.14; cf. frg. 14F. 24; 20F. 2 , 5)[22] and the apostles (p. 113.3). The name "Jesus," the title "Christ," and the collective noun "disciples" do not appear among the fragments.

The discourses in the Gospel of the Savior seem more similar to those in the Gospel of John than to the logia collections in the Sermon on the Mount (Matt 5–7), where sayings are associated only on the basis of themes or "catchwords." There are catchword and thematic connections in the Gospel of the Savior, but certain hints suggest that there may even have been a narrative sequence to the Gospel of the Savior, which would be evident if one had the complete text. For example, the savior (?) says, "Arise, let us go away from this place. For the one who will hand me over is near. And even you will flee, all of you" (p. 98.47–53). For one to leave "this place" suggests a specific location for the discourse. The reference to one who will "hand me over," suggests a plot of some sort, a reference to this figure being "near" suggests a passage of time, and the reference to the future flight indicates a plot that extends forward in time. Of course these are merely hints, but taken together they suggest that the dialogues and speeches of the Gospel of the Savior may have been contextualized in a narrative sequence.

The parallel material to this saying ("Arise, let us go away from this place. For the one who will hand me over is near") in the canonical gospels is found in connection with the passion narrative. The saying parallels Matt 26:46 (rather than Mark 14:42; see the discussion below) and John 14:31. This suggests that at least some of the discourses in the Gospel of the Savior are clearly associated with the passion narrative in Matthew. In Matt 26:46, "Rise, let us be going; see, my betrayer is at hand" comes at the end of the Gethsemane prayer segment

---

22. Twice this figure is called the "Lord" (p. 107.5, 12). In POxy 840 he is also called the savior.

(Matt 26:36–46). John has a similar saying ("Rise, let us go hence," John 14:3), but it occurs in connection with the farewell meal, and is followed by a series of farewell discourses. Thus, in terms of the narrative sequence of the canonical gospels, the discourses around p. 98 in the Gospel of the Savior seem to fall in conjunction with the last meal and/or Gethsemane.

Naming Ancient Texts

Scholars give modern titles to ancient manuscripts for several reasons: to fragmentary texts whose titles are lacking (as is the case with the Gospel of the Savior), to complete texts that were not titled in antiquity, and to texts having an ancient title in order to distinguish them from another ancient text of the same title. Sometimes texts are labeled with the place of their discovery. For example, Papyrus Oxyrhynchus 1 is the first published papyrus manuscript from the ancient Egyptian city of Oxyrhynchus. In this case the term "Oxyrhynchus" has also become the name of the series in which subsequent publications from this discovery have appeared. Egerton Papyrus 1, purchased from an antiquities dealer in Egypt, was named after the antiquities collection in which it later came to be housed. The two ancient texts in Nag Hammadi Codex V, both bearing the ancient title "The Apocalypse of James," have been renamed by modern scholars "The (First) Apocalypse of James" and "The (Second) Apocalypse of James," based on their sequence in Codex V. The sixth tractate in Nag Hammadi Codex VI lacks an ancient title and was subsequently given the title by modern scholars "The Discourse on the Eighth and Ninth" based on the subject matter of the discourse. This was also the reason for the title "On the Origin of the World" given to one of the Nag Hammadi tractates appearing twice in the collection and both times without ancient title (Nag Hammadi Codex II, 5 and XIII, 2). Sometimes ancient texts lacking titles are named after a principal character in the text, as is the case with the Gospel of Peter. In short there is currently no accepted convention for the naming of ancient texts lacking titles.* The Gospel of the Savior has been named after its principal character in the narrative. The generic designation "gospel" is in keeping with the nature of its contents.

*This is even true of the traditional titles given to the canonical New Testament texts. The letters of Paul are named after the recipients. The canonical gospels bear the names of their traditional authors. The name Hebrews is derived from the nature of the contents of the text. First, Second, and Third John are associated with the author of the Gospel of John based on certain shared concepts among all texts. Acts is titled after the type of material in the text.

On p. 100.33–48, the apostles (?) also observe a "transfiguration" of sorts, when they, upon a mountain, see the savior who had "pierced through all the heavens" (p. 100.49–51). Hence, in the Gospel of the Savior the "transfiguration scene," if that is what it is supposed to be, follows the farewell meal/Gethsemane scenes, rather than preceding them, as it does in the synoptic gospels (cf. Mark 9, 14, and par.). The reference to the crucifixion as a yet future event on p. 108.59–60 appears to set up a sequence of events for a passion story in the Gospel of the Savior that diverges from the canonical order: farewell meal/Gethsemane (p. 98), transfiguration (p. 100), and crucifixion; the latter appears to come in the missing text after p. 114.

A possible setting for another speech appears on page 100.33. The reference to the "mountain" may signal a new location in the text with language that may deliberately evoke the Mount of Transfiguration (Matt 17:1–8). In the synoptic tradition, Jesus is transfigured before the disciples and visited by the heroes of Jewish and Christian faith, Moses and Elijah.

On the other hand, if one decides that the words about the departure of the savior on p. 107.31–38 can only be used in the same context as the parallel in John 20:17–18, then the discourse on p. 107 takes on the character of a resurrection discourse, and the mountain at GSav 100.33 may be construed as the mount in Galilee (Matt 28:16), where the resurrected Jesus had directed his disciples to meet him (Matt 28:10). But since this seems to be excluded by references to the cross as future event on p. 108.59–60 and p. 114.32–37, then we must suppose that the words of the savior on p. 107.31–38 are better explained in terms of the Mount of Transfiguration.

There are references to the passing of time in the Gospel of the Savior. On frg. 5F. 23–32 (cf. p. 107.62–63) the savior says several times: "A little longer, O cross. . . . " The statement implies a related event that is anticipated in the future. The reference to the son in connection with "the third time" (p. 115.29–31) also suggests some sort of Gethsemane setting (cf. Matt 26:42–44). The discussion about Jerusalem (frg. 14F) and another unnamed geographical region (frg. 23F.5) suggest specific locations for the dialogues and discourses. These tantalizing hints at a broader narrative frame leave open the possibility that the complete text of the Gospel of the Savior might have been a narrative gospel, rather than simply a collection of sayings and/or dialogues.

Hans-Martin Schenke, on the basis of an oral report given by Hedrick at the International Coptic Congress in Münster, Germany in 1996, is the first to have called attention to the similarity between the Gospel of the Savior and other early Christian texts that have been labeled "gospels." But it is unclear whether the Gospel of the Savior is a narrative gospel like the Gospel of John, or from a dialogue/discourse gospel like certain texts in the Nag Hammadi library. In its complete form, it could easily have been a narrative gospel with extensive discourse material, such as we find in the Gospel of John. For example, if the major continuous dialogue/discourse section of the Gospel of John (12:20–18:11) is all that had been preserved of John, and this residue of John was as fragmentary as is the Gospel of the Savior, then scholars likely would have described canonical John as a "gospel" comprised of dialogues and discourses. The section 12:20–18:11 is roughly approximate to the amount of material and to the general time frame that we have preserved of the Gospel of the Savior.[23] In this hypothetical "extract" from John there is more in the way of narrative framework, but then we have all of the material from John 12:20–18:11 to examine. If slightly less material of John had been preserved, for example 13:31–17:26, there would be significantly less in the way of framework material to give a true picture of the character of the text from which the hypothetical extract had come. On the other hand, what appear to be hints at a broader narrative frame in the Gospel of the Savior may simply be due to the composite character of the text and the carelessness of its "author." In that case, the Gospel of the Savior is likely another dialogue/discourse "gospel," such as The Apocryphon of James (I,2), The Book of Thomas (II,7), The Dialogue of the Savior (III,5), or The (First) and (Second) Apocalypses of James (V,3 and 4).

It is also possible that the Gospel of the Savior is comprised of gospel-like material that was originally embedded in another text of a different genre, such as a homily or a letter, as is the case with the Epistula Apostolorum.[24] The Epistula Apostolorum contains "gospel" material set in an epistolary frame. On this assumption it might be reasonable to read some of the plural ascriptions (viz. we, us, our) in the Gospel of the Savior as figures intruding from a now lost epistolary frame. But with one possible exception[25] all these plural ascriptions are easier understood as references to the interlocutors of the savior in the Gospel of the Savior, apparently the apostles. The exception, p. 113.1–14, might conceivably reference an epistolary frame, but even it seems best understood as a somewhat longer description by one of the interlocutors in the gospel narrative. From the extant fragments of the Gospel of the Savior, however, little more may be said with certainty about the character of the complete text, or texts, from which the fragments have come.

23. John 12:20–18:11 in the Coptic New Testament represents approximately 1134 lines of Coptic text consisting of 12 letters each = 35.5 columns of 32 lines each = 18 pages of 2 columns having 32 lines per column. Or one could describe it as four sheets of parchment plus one leaf. It would be only slightly more material than we have preserved from the Gospel of the Savior.

24. This was Mirecki's initial, but tentative, assessment of the fragments in 1991. It was also suggested by Tito Orlandi at the international Coptic Congress in 1996, and by Wolf-Peter Funk in private correspondence in 1997.

25. In the following instances there is not enough context to judge: p. 121.29, 31; frg. 22H; frg. 23H.

The author clearly knows both the Matthean and Johannine traditions. There are just too many close parallels with these gospels to think otherwise. In the Gospel of the Savior, however, the canonical gospels are never quoted as literary texts. The sayings are always attributed to the savior, as is the case in the canonical gospels and other early gospel texts. Thus the authority for the sayings of Jesus in the canonical gospels is the Lord himself and not written texts, which are consciously cited as written texts. In a similar way, the Gospel of the Savior vests the authority for the sayings of the savior in the savior himself, rather than in gospels as religious texts that had achieved parity with the Jewish Bible in the faith of the church.

A quotation formula is used only once among the fragments (p. 98.63: ϥⲥⲏ2 = γέγραπται) of a passage that appears both in Zechariah (Zech 13:7), and the Gospel of Matthew (Matt 26:31; cf. Mark 14:27). The quotation in the Gospel of the Savior appears exactly as Matthew has it, however, rather than as it appears in the Coptic text of Zechariah.

GSav p. 98.63–99.3
ϥⲥⲏ2 ⲅⲁⲣ ϫⲉ †ⲛⲁⲣⲱ2̄ⲧ̄ ⲙ̄ⲡϣⲱⲥ ⲛ̄ⲥⲉϫⲱⲱⲣⲉ ⲉⲃⲟⲗ
ⲛ̄ϭⲓ ⲛ̄ⲉⲥⲟⲟⲩ ⲙ̄ⲡⲟ2ⲉ
Matt 26:31
ϥⲥⲏ2 ⲅⲁⲣ ϫⲉ †ⲛⲁⲣⲱ2̄ⲧ̄ ⲙ̄ⲡϣⲱⲥ · ⲛ̄ⲥⲉϫⲱⲱⲣⲉ ⲉⲃⲟⲗ
ⲛ̄ϭⲓ ⲛⲉⲥⲟⲟⲩ ⲙ̄ⲡⲟ2ⲉ[26]
Zech 13:7
ⲣⲱ2̄ⲧ̄ ⲙ̄ⲡϣⲱⲥ ⲁⲩⲱ ⲙⲁⲣⲟⲩϫⲱⲱⲣⲉ ⲉⲃⲟⲗ
ⲛ̄ϭⲓ ⲛⲉⲥⲟⲟⲩ[27]

The author of the Gospel of the Savior appears to be using a version of the saying known from Matthew's gospel and has woodenly included an introductory quotation formula along with the saying. None of the other New Testament parallels in the Gospel of the Savior is introduced by this standard quotation formula. And this is true of the only other exact parallel to the New Testament:

GSav p. 97.19–20
ⲛ̄ⲧⲱⲧⲛ̄ ⲡⲉ ⲡⲉ2ⲙⲟⲩ ⲙ̄ⲡⲕⲁ2
Matt 5:13
ⲛ̄ⲧⲱⲧⲛ̄ ⲡⲉ ⲡⲉ2ⲙⲟⲩ ⲙ̄ⲡⲕⲁ2[28]

Other parallels to the canonical gospel texts are similar, but not verbatim. There are numerous echoes, allusions, and close parallels in language to sayings

26. G. Horner, *The Coptic Version of the New Testament in the Southern Dialect Otherwise Called Sahidic or Thebaic*, 7 vols. (Oxford: Clarendon, 1911–24), 1.306–7. Mark 14:27 omits ⲅⲁⲣ, ⲙ̄ⲡⲟ2ⲉ, and does not use the oblique ⲛ̄ϭⲓ.

27. P. Augustini Ciasca, *Sacrorum bibliorum Fragmenta copto-sahidica Musei Borgiani iussu et sumptibus s. Congregationis de Propaganda Fide*, 2 vols.in 1 (Rome: S. Congregationis, 1885, 1889), 2.358.

28. Horner, *Coptic Version of the New Testament*, 1.32.

of Jesus in the New Testament, but only the two discussed above may be said to be identical to parallels in the Coptic New Testament. The following sayings in the Gospel of the Savior have the closest linguistic parallels with the New Testament.

1. GSav p. 98.47–51 = John 14:31, Matt 26:46, Mark 14:52
    The Gospel of the Savior has the following combined into one saying: John 14:31 ("from this place") and Matt 26:46/Mark 14:52 ("the one who will hand me over is near").[29]

2. GSav p. 98.53–55 = Matt 26:31
    The Gospel of the Savior lacks ⲧⲏⲣⲧⲛ̅ ("you all") and ϩⲛ̅ ⲧⲉⲓⲟⲩϣⲏ ("in this night").

3. GSav p. 98.60–62 = John 10:30
    The Gospel of the Savior is more emphatic by reading ⲟⲩⲁ ⲛ̅ⲟⲩⲱⲧ ("a single one").

4. GSav p. 99.3–6 = John 10:11
    The Gospel of the Savior converts into first person a phrase that appears in John 10:11 as a second-person statement.

5. GSav p. 107.31–33 = John 20:17
    The Gospel of the Savior adds an intensifying ⲛ̅ⲧⲟϥ ("indeed") and uses a temporal "Until" construction where the Coptic New Testament uses a ⲅⲁⲣ ("for") causal clause.

6. GSav p. 108.45–46 = John 16:33
    Both texts are identical only in the assertion "I have overcome the world." The Coptic New Testament also includes ⲁⲛⲟⲕ.

7. GSav p. 108.61–64 = John 19:35
    Both texts are the same except that the Gospel of the Savior renders as an imperative ("Let him bear witness") what the Coptic New Testament renders in the indicative ("he bore witness").

8. GSav p. 114.6–9 = Matt 26:39
    The Gospel of the Savior intensifies with ⲱ ("o") and reads [ⲡⲟⲧ] (in lacuna) rather than ⲭⲱ for "cup" as in the Coptic New Testament.

The author is not quoting authoritative canonical texts, since he freely recasts the material in various ways. Thus the principal religious authority for the author of the Gospel of the Savior appears to be the sayings tradition, behind which stood the personal authority of the savior.

It seems unlikely, however, that the author of the Gospel of the Savior is only drawing on the undifferentiated oral tradition from which the authors of the canonical gospels drew. The use of a narrator's aside[30] on p. 108.61–64 = John

29. The author's combining of the canonical traditions may also be the explanation for the odd statement "blood of the grape" p. 97.29–30; see the commentary.

30. See C.W. Hedrick, "Authorial Presence and Narrator in John: Commentary and Story," in J.E. Goehring, C.W. Hedrick, J.T. Sanders, with H.D. Betz, eds., *Gospel Origins and*

19:35, and what appears to be a narrative transition from a speech to an action in the canonical gospels ("Rise let us go away from this place," Matt 26:46; John 14:31 = GSav p. 98.47–51) seem to rule out this possibility. It appears that the author of the Gospel of the Savior knew the canonical gospel tradition in some form (the gospels themselves, liturgical texts, homilies, collections of logia?). Most of the parallels to the canonical tradition come from the speech material associated with the passion narrative. This may simply be due to the fact that so little of the text has been preserved, and if we had the entire text, we might find correlations to other parts of the canonical gospels as well.[31] On the other hand, one should not too quickly dismiss the idea that this text may draw, at least in part, on an oral sayings tradition, including the passion traditions.

For example, compare GSav 97.18–23 with Matt 5:13–15, where the Gospel of the Savior and Matthew share two sayings. But what appears in the Gospel of the Savior as a saying with two parallel members ("You are the salt of the earth; you are the lamp that illuminates the world") appears in Matthew as two individual sayings, each followed by an interpretive expansion: 5:13a followed by 5:13b and 5:14a followed by 5:14b–16. In this one instance, it is at least possible that both texts have appropriated a double stich saying from oral tradition. The Gospel of the Savior uses it as a double stich saying but Matthew breaks it up by adding clarifying expansion to each stich.

The Gospel of the Savior also shares a saying with the Coptic Gospel of Thomas that is unknown to the canonical gospels. This clearly indicates that both author's sources are not limited to the canonical literature.

GSav p. 107.43–48:

ⲡ[ⲉⲧϨⲏⲚ] ⲉϨⲟⲩⲚ ⲉⲣⲟ[ⲓ̈ ⲉϥ]ϨⲏⲚ ⲉϨⲟⲩⲚ ⲉ[ⲡⲕ]ⲱϨⲏⲦ̄
ⲡⲉⲧⲟⲩⲏⲩ ⲉⲃⲟⲗ ⲙ̄ⲙⲟⲓ ⲉϥⲟⲩⲏⲩ ⲉⲃⲟⲗ ⲙ̄ⲡⲱⲛϨ

GThom 82:

ⲡⲉⲧϨⲏⲚ ⲉⲣⲟⲉⲓ ⲉϥϨⲏⲚ ⲉⲧⲥⲁⲧⲉ ⲁⲩⲱ
ⲡⲉⲧⲟⲩⲏⲩ ⲙ̄ⲙⲟⲉⲓ ϥⲟⲩⲏⲩ ⲛ̄ⲧⲙⲛ̄ⲧⲉⲣⲟ

The sayings are the same except for certain syntactic variants (omission of ⲉϨⲟⲩⲚ and ⲉⲃⲟⲗ in the Thomas version of the saying), and one variant in substance. The Gospel of the Savior reads at the end of the second stich "life," instead of "kingdom," as it appears in the Gospel of Thomas. This saying is known as a saying of Jesus in its Gospel of Thomas version (i.e., kingdom instead of life), in Origen (HomJer 20.3), and Didymus the Blind (Migne, *PG*, 39, 1488D). Neither of these two parallels appears to draw on the Gospel of

Christian Beginnings. In Honor of J.M. Robinson (Sonoma, Calif.: Polebridge Press, 1990), 74–93.

31. This is similar to the Gospel of Peter. It is fragmentary and, like the Gospel of the Savior, contains only passion material in its extant fragments.

Thomas as a literary document.[32] The saying also appears as a saying of Jesus in its Gospel of the Savior version (i.e., life instead of kingdom) in a fourth century Armenian text, "Exposition of the Gospel,"[33] but there is no indication of a literary relationship between the Gospel of the Savior and the Armenian text. Hence it appears that the differences between the sayings are due to independent acquisition from the oral tradition by Origen, the Armenian text, and the Gospel of the Savior, or perhaps due to a free interchange of language: entering the kingdom is equivalent to entering life.[34] The most probable explanation for the way all three texts have come by this saying, however, is that each represents an independent performance of a saying acquired from the oral tradition.

Such a conclusion suggests that the Gospel of the Savior was composed at a time when Christian oral traditions were still as influential as written gospel texts. Thus the latest date for the composition of the Gospel of the Savior that best fits these conditions is the latter half of the second century before the canonical gospels had consolidated their influence over the church, and at which time the oral tradition remained a viable competitor to the written texts; but it is scarcely possible to be certain.

There are also some close parallels between the Gospel of the Savior and the Strasbourg Coptic Papyrus that are particularly striking in two such highly fragmentary texts.[35]

1. Coptic 5 (Recto): series of statements followed by "Amen"; cf. GSav 105.7–43; 108.17–64.
2. Coptic 5 (Recto): "I am become King" (line 13); cf. GSav 108.17–19.
3. Coptic 5 (Verso): the setting appears to be Gethsemane; cf. GSav 114.6–9, 59–61; 115. 29–31
4. Coptic 5 (Verso): "[overcome] the world" (lines 23–24); cf. GSav 108.45–49
5. Coptic 5 (Verso): Jesus dialogues with the apostles (lines 3, 9, 10, 14, 19–20; cf. GSav 107.3–25; 113.2–16.

---

32. See C.W. Hedrick, *Parables as Poetic Fictions. The Creative Voice of Jesus* (Peabody, Mass.: Hedrickson, 1994), 240–41.

33. Joseph Schäfers, *Eine altsyrische antimarkionitische Erklärung von Parabeln des Herrn und Zwei andere altsyrische Abhandlungen zu Texten des Evangeliums mit Beiträgen zu Tatians Diatessaron und Markions Neuem Testament* (Neutestamentliche Abhandlungen 6.1–2; Münster: Aschendorf, 1917), 79. See page 185 for Schäfers' Greek retroversion, and compare the translation of G. Eagen, *Saint Ephrem. An Exposition of the Gospel* (CSCO 5 and 6; Louvain: Secrétarit CSCO, 1968), 6.62.

34. See C.W. Hedrick, "The Gospel of Thomas and Early Christian Tradition" in Søren Giversen and Marianne A. Skovmand, eds., *Essays on Early Christian Tradition Presented at the University of Aarhus; Aarhus, Denmark* (to appear; the title of the volume is tentative).

35. Ádolf Jacoby, *Ein neues Evangelienfragment* (Strassburg: Karl Trübner, 1900); Schneemelcher and Wilson, *New Testament Apocrypha*, 1.103–105.

6. Coptic 6 (Recto): p. 157; "apostleship": (line 4), and Coptic 6 (Verso): p. 158: "apostle[ship]" (lines 5–6); cf. GSav 113.12.
7. Coptic 6 (Recto): p. 157: "reveal to you all my glory" (lines 1–2); cf. GSav 107.10–23.
8. Coptic 6 (Verso): p. 158: "our eyes penetrated all places" (line 1); cf. GSav 100.36–38.

The author stands in a tradition of Christian pluralism, and was influenced by ideas that have come to be associated with Gnosticism and apocalyptic, though it is not possible to identify these ideas and influences with the fully developed gnostic systems of the second century. Gnostic motifs in the Gospel of the Savior are simply too general to allow such an identification. The author has a decided preference for orthodox Christian traditions (for example, the descent into Hell: p. 97.59–63; the Jesus sayings tradition; and the Eucharist: p. 105.11–14) but, like the canonical gospels and Paul, the author is also influenced by speculative thought that came to be characteristic of Gnosticism of the second century. There is no evidence, however, of the type of cosmic speculation like that found in Zostrianos (Nag Hammadi Codex VIII,*1*), on the one hand, or the religious-philosophical thought one finds in Allogenes (Nag Hammadi Codex XI,3), on the other. Nor is there evidence that would allow the text to be associated with any particular second-century gnostic movement.

There are references to heavenly journeys (p. 100.33–51; p. 113.13–16, 24–28, 38–43, 56–57); but heavenly journeys are not specifically gnostic. Rather they are part of the general religious speculation of the ancient world, and are rather widespread in antiquity, particularly in apocalyptic literature.[36] The genre is used in a broad variety of texts (cf. 2 Cor 12:1–4, for example). Other "gnostic" features are even more general:

1. "Do not let matter (ὕλη) rule over you" (p. 98.45–46).
2. The apostles say: "As for us apostles, this world became as the darkness [before] us. We became as [those] among the Aeons of glory" (p. 113.3–8).
3. The savior says: "[A little longer], O (ὦ) cross (σταυρός), and that which is lacking is perfected, and that which is diminished is full. A little longer, O (ὦ) cross (σταυρός), and that which [fell] arises. A [little longer], O (ὦ) cross (σταυρός), and all the Pleroma (πλήρωμα) is perfected" (5F.22–32).
4. "Oh my holy members (μέλος), my seeds (σπέρμα) who are blessed" (p. 100.3–5).

---

36. See James D. Tabor, "Heaven, Ascent to" in D. N. Freedman, et al., eds., *The Anchor Bible Dictionary* (New York: Doubleday, 1992), 3.91–94.

Other than these features, the extant fragments of the Gospel of the Savior place it in the context of a Christian pluralism that has not yet been crowded out by an emerging ecclesiasticism, which was privileged by the conversion of Constantine in the fourth century. There are no obvious ecclesiastical concerns reflected among the fragments, although one exception may be the highly fragmentary section at p. 116.31 (see the commentary).

Gospel
of the
Savior

[q̄z̄]

1–5	[	33	[ⲉⲓⲥ
6	[.]ⲉ . [	34–54	[
7	[.]ⲍⲉ[		
8	[.]ⲍⲟⲩ . [		
9	[.]ⲟⲛⲁⲁ[6± ⲧⲙ]		
10	ⲛ̄ⲧⲉⲣⲟ ⲧⲁ[		
11	ⲟⲩⲉ · ⲛϣⲁ[		
12	ⲙⲓⲧ ⲙⲡⲉⲉ . [		
13	ⲣⲉ ⲧⲙⲛ̄ⲧⲉⲣⲟ ⲛ̄[ⲙ]		
14	ⲡⲏⲩⲉ ⲛ̄ⲥⲁ ⲟⲩⲛⲁⲙ		
15	ⲙ̄ⲙⲱⲧⲛ̄· ⲛⲁⲓ̈ⲁⲧϥ		
16	ⲙ̄ⲡⲉⲧⲛⲁⲟⲩⲱⲙ		
17	ⲛⲙ̄ⲙⲁⲓ̈ ⲍⲛ̄ ⲧⲙⲛ̄ⲧ		
18	ⲉⲣⲟ ⲛ̄ⲙⲡⲏⲩⲉ· ⲛ̄		
19	ⲧⲱⲧⲛ̄ ⲡⲉ ⲡⲉⲍⲙⲟⲩ		
20	ⲙ̄ⲡⲕⲁⲍ ⲁⲩⲱ ⲛ̄ⲧⲱ		
21	ⲧⲛ̄ ⲡⲉ ⲧⲗⲁⲙⲡⲁⲥ		
22	ⲉⲧⲣ̄ⲟⲩⲟⲉⲓⲛ ⲉⲡⲕⲟ		
23	ⲥⲙⲟⲥ· ⲙ̄ⲡⲣ̄ⲍⲓⲛⲏ[ⲃ]	55	[ ] . [
24	ⲟⲩⲇⲉ ⲙ̄ⲡⲣ̄ϫⲓ ⲣⲕ	56	[.] . ⲛⲛⲉ . . [
25	ⲣⲓⲕⲉ ϣ[. . .] ⲉⲧⲁ	57	ⲉϣϫⲉ ⲛⲁⲡⲕⲟⲥⲙ[ⲟⲥ]
26	ⲉ . . . ⲧ . . . . ⲛ ⲙ̄	58	ⲁⲓ̈ⲑⲉⲣⲁⲡⲉⲩⲉ [ⲙ̄ⲙⲟ]
27	ⲡⲉⲛⲇⲩⲙⲁ ⲛ̄ⲧⲙⲛ	59	ⲟⲩ· ϣϣⲉ ⲉⲣⲟⲓ̈ ⲟⲛ
28	ⲧⲉⲣⲟ ⲡⲁⲓ̈ ⲉⲛⲧⲁⲓ̈	60	ⲉⲃⲱⲕ ⲉⲡⲉⲥⲛⲧ ⲉ
29	ϣⲟⲡϥ ⲍⲙ̄ ⲡⲉⲥⲛⲟϥ	61	ⲁⲙⲛ̄ⲧⲉ ⲉⲧⲃⲉ ⲛ̄ⲯ[ⲩⲭⲟ]
30	ⲙ̄ⲡⲉⲗⲟⲟⲗⲉ: ⲁϥ	62	ⲟⲩⲉ ⲉⲧⲙⲏⲣ ⲍⲙ̄ ⲡ
31	ⲟⲩⲟϣⲃϥ ⲛ̄ϭⲓ ⲁⲛⲇⲣⲉ	63	ⲙⲁ ⲉⲧⲙ̄ⲙⲁⲩ ⲧⲉ
32	[ⲁ]ⲥ ⲡⲉϫⲁϥ ϫⲉ ⲡⲁⲭⲟ	64	ⲛⲟⲩ ⲟ̄ⲉ ⲡⲉⲧⲉϣϣⲉ[

29 ⲟ² written above the line.

[97]

1–7	[	33–56	[

8   **1** [the]

9   kingdom [

10–12 [

13   [**2**] the kingdom of [the]

14   heavens at your (pl.) right

15   hand. ³Blessed is

16   [the one] who will eat

17   with me in the

18   [kingdom] of the heavens.

19   ⁴You (pl.) are the salt

20   of the earth, and you (pl.)

21   are the lamp ($\lambda\alpha\mu\pi\acute{\alpha}s$)

22   that illuminates the world

      ($\kappa\acute{o}\sigma\mu os$).

23   ⁵Do not sleep

24   nor ($o\grave{v}\delta\acute{\epsilon}$) [slumber

25   [

26   [**6**   ] in

27   the garment ($\check{\epsilon}\nu\delta\nu\mu\alpha$) of the

28   kingdom, which (i.e., garment) I

29   bought with the blood

30   of the grape: ⁷Andrew

31   replied to him.

32   [He] said, "My [Lord]

57   **2** If I have cared for

      ($\theta\epsilon\rho\alpha\pi\epsilon\nu\hat{\epsilon}\nu$)

58   the things of the world ($\kappa\acute{o}\sigma\mu os$),

59   it is also fitting for me

60   to go down to

61   Hades because of [the souls

      ($\psi\nu\chi\acute{\eta}$)]

62   that are bound in

63   that place. ²Now

64   therefore, what is fitting [

13, 18 "heavens": cf. the usage in the Gospel of Matthew.   **13–14** Mark 10:37, 40;
Matt 20:21.   **15–18** Luke 14:15; 22:29–30; Matt 8:11; Luke 13:29; cf. Matt
20:23.   **19–20** Matt 5:13.   **20–22** Matt 5:14–15; cf. John 8:12, GThom 10 (NHC
II,2:34,14–16).   **28–30** Mark 14:23–25; Matt 26:27–29; Luke 22:18–20; cf. Gen
49:11; Deut 32:14; Sir 39:26, 50:15.   **30** "grape" perhaps: "vine."
57 Perhaps: "attended to."   **59–61** I Pet 3:19; Iren, AdvHaer 5.31.1–2; GPet.
10:4–5 (Miller).

[qH]

1–22	[		

33	[ⲡⲉ
34–37	[
38	[ ] · · [
39	[ ]ⲟⳅ · [
40	[ ]ⲁϣⲁⲣ[·]
41	[ ]ⲩ ⲉⲣ̄ⲭⲟ[·]
42	[· · · ·]ⲧⲉⲛⲟⲩ ⲋⲉ
43	[ⲉⲛⳅⲟ]ⲥⲟⲛ ⲧⲉⲧⲛ̄
44	[ϣⲟⲟ]ⲡ ⳅⲙ̄ ⲡⲥⲱⲙ[ⲁ]
45	ⲙ̄ⲡⲣ̄ⲧⲣⲉⲑⲩⲗⲏ ⲣ̄
46	ϫⲟⲉⲓⲥ ⲉⲣⲱⲧⲛ̄ :
47	ⲧⲱⲟⲩⲛ ⲙⲁⲣⲟⲛ ⲉ
48	ⲃⲟⲗ ⳅⲙ̄ ⲡⲉⲓ̈ⲙⲁ · ⲁϥ
49	ⳅⲱⲛ ⲅⲁⲣ · ⲉⳅⲟⲩⲛ ⲛ̄
50	ϭⲓ ⲡⲉⲧⲛⲁⲡⲁⲣⲁⲇⲓ
51	ⲇⲟⲩ ⲙ̄ⲙⲟⲓ̈ · ⲁⲩⲱ
52	ⲛ̄ⲧⲱⲧⲛ̄ ⲧⲉⲧⲛⲁ
53	ⲡⲱⲧ ⲧⲏⲣ̄ⲧⲛ̄ ⲛ̄ⲧⲉ
54	ⲧⲛ̄ⲥⲕⲁⲛⲇⲁⲗⲓⳅⲉ
55	ⲛ̄ⳅⲏⲧ · ⲧⲉⲧⲛ̄ⲁ
56	ⲡⲱⲧ ⲧⲏⲣ̄ⲧⲛ̄ ⲛ̄ⲧⲉ
57	[ⲧ]ⲛ̄ⲕ[ⲁⲁⲧ] ⲙⲁⲩⲁⲁⲧ
58	ⲁⲗⲗⲁ ⲛ̄ ⲧ̄ϭⲉⲉⲧ ⲙⲁⲩ
59	ⲁⲁⲧ ⲁⲛ ϫⲉ ⲡⲁⲓ̈ⲱⲧ
60	ϣⲟⲟⲡ ⲛ̄ⲙⲙⲁⲓ̈ · ⲁ
61	ⲛⲟⲕ ⲙⲛ̄ ⲡⲁⲓ̈ⲱⲧ ⲁ
62	ⲛⲟⲛ ⲟⲩⲁ ⲛ̄ⲟⲩⲱⲧ ·
63	ϥⲥⲏⳅ ⲅⲁⲣ ϫⲉ ϯⲛⲁ
64	ⲣⲱⳅⲧ ⲙ̄ⲡϣⲱⲥ ⲛ̄

23	[ ] · · ϣ[
24	[ⳅ]ⲱⲃ ⲛⲓⲙ ⳅⲛ̄ ⲟⲩ[ⲱ]
25	ⲣ̣ϫ · ⲁⲛⲟⲕ ⳅⲱ ϯⲛⲁ
26	ϭⲱⲗ̄ⲡ ⲛⲏⲧⲛ̄ ⲉⲃⲟⲗ
27	ⳅⲛ̄ ⲟⲩⲣⲁϣⲉ · ϯⲥⲟ
28	ⲟⲩⲛ ⲅⲁⲣ ϫⲉ ⲟⲩⲛ̄ϣ
29	ϭⲟⲙ ⲙ̄ⲙⲱⲧⲛ̄ ⲉⲣ
30	ⳅⲱⲃ ⲛⲓⲙ ⳅⲛ̄ ⲟⲩⲣⲁ
31	ϣⲉ · ⲡⲣⲱⲙⲉ ⲅⲁⲣ
32	ⲟⲩⲁⲩⲧⲟⳅⲟⲩⲥⲓⲟⲥ

32 ⲁⲩⲧⲟⳅⲟⲩⲥⲓⲟⲥ for: ⲁⲩⲧⲉⳅⲟⲩⲥⲓⲟⲥ .   41 ⲟ perhaps: ⲥ̣.

[98]

1–23 [

24 **3** everything with
25 [assurance]. 2I myself will
26 reveal to you (pl.)

27 with joy. 3For (γάρ)
28 I know that you (pl.)
29 are able to do
30 everything with joy.
31 4For (γάρ) the person
32 [is] unconditionally free
(αὐτεξούσιος)

33–41 [
42 **4** [   ] now therefore
43 [while (ὅσον)] you (pl.)
44 [are] in the body (σῶμα),
45 do not let matter (ὕλη)
46 rule over you (pl.):
47 2Arise, let us
48 go away from this place. For
(γάρ)
49 the one who will
50 hand me over (παραδιδόναι)
51 is near. 3And
52 even you (pl.) will
53 flee, all of you (pl.). 4And you
(pl.) will be
54 offended (σκανδαλίζειν)
55 by me. 5You (pl.) will
56 flee, all of you (pl.), and
57 [will leave me] alone,
58 but (ἀλλά) I do not remain
alone
59 for my Father
60 is with me.6 I
61 and my Father,
62 we are a single one.
63 7For (γάρ) it is written "I will
64 strike the shepherd and

28–30 Cf. Luke 9:1, par.; Luke 24:49.   **31** "person" perhaps: "the man."
47–48 John 14:31; Mark 14:42; Matt 26:46.   **49–51** Mark 14:42; Matt
26:46.   **53–55** Matt 26:31; cf. Mark 14:27.   **55–56** Matt 26:56; Mark
14:50.   **61–62** John 10:30; cf. 17:21.   **63** to p. 99.3; Zech 13:7; Matt 26:31;
Mark 14:27.

q̄ⲑ̇

1   ⲥⲉⲭⲱⲱⲣⲉ ⲉⲃⲟⲗ
2   ⲛ̄ϭⲓ ⲛⲉⲥⲟⲟⲩ ⲙ̄ⲡⲟ
3   ⲍⲉ· ⲁⲛⲟⲕ ϭⲉ ⲡⲉ
4   ⲡϣⲱⲥ ⲉⲧⲛⲁⲛⲟⲩϥ
5   ϯⲛⲁⲕⲱ ⲛ̄ⲧⲁⲯⲩⲭⲏ
6   ⲍⲁⲣⲱⲧⲛ̄[·] ⲛ̄ⲧⲱⲧⲛ̄
7   ⲍⲱⲧ ⲧⲏⲩⲧⲛ̄ ⲕⲱ
8   ⲛ̄ⲛⲉⲧⲙ̄ⲯⲩⲭⲏ ⲍⲁ
9   ⲛⲉⲧⲛ̄ϣⲃⲉ[ⲉⲣ]ⲉ ⲭⲉ
10 ⲕⲁⲥ [ⲉ]ⲧⲉⲧⲛⲉⲣ̄ⲁ
11 ⲛⲁϥ ⲙ̄ⲡⲁⲓ̈ⲱⲧ· ⲭⲉ
12 ⲙ̄ⲛ ⲉⲛⲧⲟⲗⲏ ⲉⲛ[ⲁ]
13 ⲁⲁϥ ⲉⲧⲁⲓ̈ ⲉⲧⲣⲁ
14 ⲕⲱ ⲛ̄ⲧⲁⲯⲩⲭⲏ [ⲍⲁ ⲛ]
15 ⲣⲱ[ⲙ]ⲉ ⲉⲧⲃⲉ [ⲡⲁⲓ̈]
16 ⲡⲁⲓ̈ⲱⲧ ⲙⲉ ⲙⲙⲟⲓ̈ ⲭⲉ
17 ⲁⲓ̈ⲭⲱⲕ ⲉⲃⲟⲗ ⲙ̄ⲡⲉϥ
18 ⲟⲩⲱϣ· ⲭⲉ ⲁⲛ[ⲅ̄ ⲟⲩ]
19 ⲛⲟⲩⲧⲉ ⲁⲓ̈ⲣ̄ⲣⲱ[ⲙⲉ]
20 ⲉⲧⲃⲉ . [
21 ⲟⲩⲁⲧ[
22 ⲧⲉ . [
23 ⲣⲟ ⲛ̄[
24 ⲧⲉⲛ[
25 ⲛ̄ⲧⲉ[
26 . . [
27–32 [

33 ⲙⲛ̄ⲛⲥⲁ ⲟⲩⲏⲣ ⲛ̄ⲟ[ⲩ]
34 ⲟⲉⲓϣ· ⲏ̄ ⲙ̄ⲙⲟⲛ ⲛ̄ⲅ
35 ⲣ̄ ⲡⲉⲛⲙⲉⲉⲩⲉ ⲛ̄ⲅ[ⲧⲛ̄]
36 ⲛⲟⲟⲩ ⲛ̄ⲥⲱⲛ, ⲛ̄ⲅⲛ
37 ⲧⲛ̄ ⲉⲃⲟⲗ ⲍ̄ⲙ ⲡⲕⲟ
38 ⲥⲙⲟ[ⲥ · ⲛ̄]ⲧ̄ⲛⲉⲓ ϣⲁ
39 ⲣⲟⲕ[. . .]ϥ . [.]¯¯
40 ⲧⲛ̄[
41 . [
42–63 [

64   [ⲍ̄ⲛ]

99

1	[they] will be scattered,
2	namely, the sheep of the
3	flock." 8Yet I am
4	the good shepherd.
5	9I will lay down my life (ψυχή)
6	for you (pl.). You (pl.)
7	yourselves also lay down
8	your (pl.) lives (ψυχή) for
9	your (pl.) friends in
10	order that you (pl.) might be
11	pleasing to my Father. 10For
12	no commandment (ἐντολή)
13	is greater than this, that I
14	lay down my life (ψυχή) [for]
15	people. 11Because of [this]
16	my Father loves me, for
17	I completed [his]
18	will. 12For (although) I [was]
19	divine, I became [human]
20	because [
21–32	[

33	**5** after how much
34	time? 2Or (ἤ) if not, [will you (sg.)]
35	remember us, summon
36	us, and take
37	us out of the world (κόσμος),
38	[that] we may come to
39	you (sg.)? [
40–63	

64	**6** [	by]

1–3 Matt 26:31=Mark 14:27.   **3–6** John 10:11.   **6–9** John 15:13.
11–13 Mark 12:31.   **13–15** John 10:15–18; 15:13.   **15** "people" perhaps: "men."
18–19 Cf. John 1:1–18; Phil 2:6–11.   **19** "[Human]" perhaps: "man."

P̄

1	OYN⟦O⟧`A´Y· ΠCⲰTHP
2	ΠEXAϥ NAN· XE
3	ⲱ̂ NAMEⲖOC ET
4	OYAAB` NACΠEP
5	MA ETCMAMA
6	AT . TⲰ . [.] . N̄TE
7	ϥ[. .] . E[. . .] . XE
8	[ ]ⲰⲖHⲖ
9	[ ]·
10–32	[

33	EXM̄ ΠTOOY AN[ON]
34	ⲞⲰⲰN ANⲢⲐE N̄
35	NICⲰMA M̄ΠN̄Ā·
36	ANENBAⲖ OYⲰN N̄
37	CACA NIM· AΠMA
38	THⲢϥ̄ ϬⲰⲖⲠ̄ EBOⲖ
39	M̄ΠENM̄TO EBOⲖ·
40	AN⳿Ⲟ[Ⲱ]N EMΠHYE
41	AYT[Ⲱ]ⲰN E[⳿Ⲟ]ⲢAⲒ N
42	CA NEYEⲢ[H]Y· NET
43	ⲢOEIC EMΠYⲖH AY
44	ⲰTOⲢT̄Ⲣ· ANAⲄ
45	ⲄEⲖOC Ⲣ̄ ⲞOTE AY
46	[Π]ⲰT⳿ EΠI[.] . M̄ . . .
47	[AY]MEEYE [X]E EY
48	NABⲰⲖ⳿ EBOⲖ TH
49	ⲢOY· ANNAY EΠE(N)
50	[C]ⲰTHⲢ⳿ EAϥXⲰTE
51	[⳿N̄] M̄ΠHYE THⲢOY·
52	[5± O]YEⲢHTE
53	[8±]M̄ΠTO
54	[9±]EⲢE
55	[9±]TE N̄
56	[7±]E M̄ΠE .
57	[8±]AAⲢ̄
58	[10±] . E
59–64	[

---

1 Y² O corrected to Y. A written above Y. Apparently the scribe started to write OYNOY, stopped at O², erased it, and wrote Y with A above Y.   **6** .¹ perhaps: A, Λ, X, A.   **33** E crowded at the beginning of the line.

100

1   sight. 2The savior (σωτήρ)

2   said to us:

3   "O (ὦ) my holy

4   members (μέλος), my seeds
    (σπέρμα)

5   who are blessed

6–7   [

8   [   ] pray

9–32   [

33   7 upon the mountain and we

34   too became like

35   the spiritual (πνεῦμα) bodies
     (σῶμα).

36   2Our eyes opened up to

37   every side, and the entire

38   place was revealed

39   before us.

40   3We [approached] the heavens,

41   and they [rose] up against

42   each other. 4Those who

43   watch the gates (πύλη)

44   were disturbed. 5The angels
     (ἄγγελος)

45   were afraid, and they

46   [fled] to the [

47   [They] thought [that] they

48   would all be destroyed.

49   6We saw our

50   savior (σωτήρ) after he pierced

51   [through] all the heavens.

52   [7   ] foot

53   [   ] of the

54–64   [

3–4 ⲙⲉⲗⲟⲥ cf. GSav, 107.50–51 and GSav, frg. 9H.4–5; cf. 1 Cor 6:15; 12:27; John 15:5. **33** Cf. Mark 9:2–4; Matt 17:1–3; Luke 9:28–29(?); GPhil NHC II,3: 58, 5–10. **35** Cf. 1 Cor 15:35–50. **36–37** Cf. Strasbourg Coptic Papyrus 6 (verso): p. 158.

[P̄Є]

1–2	[	33–38	[
3	. [		
4	₂ . [ⲡⲉ]		
5	ⲧⲛⲁ[		
6	ϯⲛⲁ[. . .] . ⲙ̄ⲙ[ⲟϥ]		
7	ϩⲱ ϩ[ⲁⲙⲏ]ⲛ· ⲡⲉ(ⲛ)	39	ⲡⲟ . [
8	ⲧⲁϥ . [.] . ⲉⲣⲟ·ⲓ ⲁ	40	ⲛ̄ⲧⲕ̄ ⲡ[
9	ⲛⲟⲕ [. . .] ϯⲛⲁⲧⲣⲉϥ	41	ⲝⲓⲛⲧⲁ[
10	. [. .] ⲛⲙ̄ⲙⲁ·ⲓ ϩⲁ	42	ⲥ̄ⲣ̄ⲟ̄ⲥ̄ [
11	ⲙ[ⲏ]ⲛ ᵛᵃᶜᵃᵗ ⲡⲉⲧⲉ ⲛ̄[ϥ]	43	ϩⲁⲙⲏⲛ· . [. . . .]
12	ⲝ[ⲓ] ⲁⲛ ⲙ̄ⲡⲁⲥⲱⲙ[ⲁ]	44	ϩⲓ ϩⲁ[ⲓ]ⲃⲉⲥ ϩ[ⲓ.ⲭⲱ⸗]
13	[ⲙ̄]ⲛ ⲡⲁⲥⲛⲟϥ· ⲡⲁ[·ⲓ]	45	[ⲛ̄]ϭⲓ ⲛⲉⲧϩⲓⲟⲩ[ⲛⲁⲙ]
14	ⲟⲩ ϣ̄ⲙ̄ⲙⲟ ⲉⲣⲟ·ⲓ ⲡⲉ	46	ⲁ[ⲭ]ⲛ̄ ⲛⲉⲧϩⲓϩ[ⲃⲟⲩⲣ]
15	ϩⲁⲙ[ⲏ]ⲛ· . [. .] . ⲉⲣⲟϥ	47	[. . .]ⲥ̄ⲣ̄ⲟ̄ⲥ̄ ⲛ[
16	ⲝⲱⲕ [. .] . [	48	[. . .]ⲛⲁⲃⲱⲗ ⲉ[ⲃⲟⲗ]
17	ⲝⲟ[	49	[7±] . ⲝⲉ[
18	ⲛ̄ⲥⲱ[	50–64	[
19–32	[		

The bottom part of this page may be frg. 5H.   **45** [ⲛ̄] appears to have been written into the left margin; see p. 105.5, 8, 12, 16.

[105]

1–3　[

4　　**8** [　　the one who]

5　　will [

6　　I will [　　him]

7　　[myself. Amen]. **2**The one

8　　who [　　] to me

9　　I [　　] I will cause him

10　　[　　] with me. Amen.

11　　[　　] **3**The one who does

12　　not receive my body (σῶμα)

13　　[and] my blood, [this one]

14　　is a stranger to me.

15　　Amen. [**4**　　] to him

16　　complete [

17–32　[

33–39 [

40　　**9** You (sg.) are the [

41　　since [

42　　cross (σταυρός) [

43　　Amen. [**2**

44　　cast a shadow [over　　]

45　　namely, those on (the) [right]

46　　[apart from] those on (the) [left]

47　　[　　　　] cross (σταυρός)

48　　[　　　　] will release

49　　[　　　　] for [

50–64 [

11–13 Cf. Mark 14:22–24; Matt 26:26–28; Luke 22:19–20; John 6:51–58.
15 Amen: cf. the hymn in the AcJohn 94–96.

[P̄S̄]

1–6 [	33–35 [
	36 [10±] . є
	37 [10±] . n
	38 [9±]ωвє·
7 [8±]n̄мпа	39 [.] . n . [5±]n аү
8 [8±]ϣагє	40 бωϣт [єво]λ ҙнтк̄:
9 [. . . . м̄п̄р̄]рıмє ω̄	41 оүа єϥ[сωв]є аүω
10 [6±] алла ра	42 єϥраϣє [к]єоүа
11 [ϣє n̄]тоϥ n̄гсоү(n)	43 єϥрıмє є[ϥҙнв]є
12 [. . .]х̣оєıс єϥn . [	44 аүω єϥнєҙпє [ак]
13 [. . .] . к· хє оүр̄ . [	45 [ϣ]орпк̄ єроï ω̄ [п]є
14 [. . .]пє аүω єϥє[	46 с̄р̄о̄с̄ анок ҙ[ωωт]
15 [.] . ү ҙамн[n . . . т]	47 †наϣорп̄т єрок
16 мєҙснтє[	48 n̄ . [.] кω м̄[.] аïω
17 а м̄[	49 [8±]о̣n ҙє(n)
18–32 [	50 [8±]о̣n ҙє(n)
	51 [ ]єn . n
	52–64 [

The bottom part of this page may be 5F.   **10** Possibly [пєс̄р̄о̄с̄]; мєлос usually
appears with a modifier; cf. GSav 107.50–51; GSav 100.3–4; GSav 9H. 4–5. A singular rather than plural is required in line 10 because of n̄г line 11.   **12** Trace of ink at
the end of the line is characteristic of ı, н, n.   **13** Letter at the beginning of the line is
characteristic of о, ω.   **13–14** Perhaps: оүр̄м/[мао] пє.   **38** Perhaps: с]ωвє .
45, 47 ϣорп≠ translates a metaphorical use of the Greek verb ὀρθρίζειν; cf. Jer 25:3
(LXX).

[106]

1–8 [

9   **10** [Do not] weep, O (ὦ̂),
10   [   ], but (ἀλλά)
11   rather rejoice, and understand
12   [   ] Lord, since he [
13   [   ]. 2For [
14   [   ] and [he will
15   [   ] Amen. [3   the]
16   second [

17–32 [

33–38 [

39   **11** [   ] they
40   looked toward you (sg.),
41   one [mocking] and
42   deriding; another
43   weeping, [mourning],
44   and [wailing. 2You (sg.) were]
45   eager for me, O (ὦ̂)
46   cross (σταυρός); I also
47   will be eager for you (sg.).

48–64 [

---

40 "you"; probably the cross (cf. line 46).   **41–44** Mark 15:18–20, 29–31; Matt 27:29–31, 39–41; Luke 23:27, 48.   **44–47** Cf. Mark 14:32–36, par.; ApocPet NHC VII,3:81,3–24; 82, 27–83,3; AcAndrew 349 (Hennecke-Schneemelcher-Wilson, 2.148).   **45, 47** Lit.: "to be earlier than."

P̄Z̄

1	[. . . .]ⲛⲁⲩ ⲉⲣⲟⲟⲩ·	33	ϩⲣⲁⲓ̈ ϣⲁ [ⲡ]ⲁⲓ̈ⲱ[ⲧ ⲉ]
2	ⲙ̄[ⲡ̄ⲣ̄ⲱⲧⲟ]ⲣⲧ̄ⲣ ϭⲉ	34	ⲧⲉ ⲡⲉⲧ[ⲛ̄ⲓ̈]ⲱⲧ [ⲡⲉ]
3	ⲉⲧⲉ[ⲧⲛ̄]ϣⲁⲛⲛⲁⲩ	35	ⲁⲩⲱ ⲡ[ⲁⲛⲟⲩⲧⲉ ⲉ]
4	ⲉⲣⲟⲓ̈ [·]ⲡⲉϫⲁⲛ ⲛⲁⲋ	36	ⲧⲉ ⲡⲉⲧⲛ̄ⲛⲟⲩⲧⲉ ⲡⲉ
5	ϫⲉ ⲡϫ[ⲟ]ⲉⲓⲥ ⲉⲕⲛⲁ	37	ⲁⲩⲱ ⲡⲁϫⲟⲉⲓⲥ ⲉⲧⲉ
6	ⲟⲩⲟⲛ[ϩ]ⲕ ⲉⲣⲟⲛ ⲛ̄	38	ⲡⲉⲧⲛ̄ϫⲟⲉⲓⲥ ⲡⲉ·
7	[ⲁ]ϣ ⲛ̄ⲥⲙⲟⲧ ⲏ̂ ⲉⲕ	39	ⲉϣⲱⲡⲉ ⲇⲉ ⲉⲣϣⲁ(ⲛ)
8	[ⲛ]ⲁⲉⲓ ϩⲛ̄ ⲁϣ ⲛ̄ⲥⲱ	40	ⲟⲩⲁ̓ ϩⲱ[ⲛ] ⲉϩⲟ[ⲩⲛ]
9	[ⲙ]ⲁ ⲙⲁⲧⲁⲙⲟⲛ:	41	ⲉⲣⲟⲓ̈ ϥⲛⲁ[ⲣ]ⲱ[ⲕ]ϩ̄
10	[ⲁ]ϥⲟⲩⲱ̄ϣ̄ⲃ̄ ⲛ̄ϭⲓ ⲓ̈ⲱ	42	[ⲁ]ⲛⲟⲕ ⲡⲉ ⲡⲕ[ⲱ]ϩ̄ⲧ̄
11	ϩⲁⲛⲛⲏⲥ ⲡⲉϫⲁϥ·	43	[ⲉ]ⲧϫⲉⲣⲟ· ⲡ[ⲉⲧϩⲏⲛ]
12	ϫⲉ ⲡϫⲟⲉⲓⲥ᾽ ⲉⲕϣⲁ(ⲛ)	44	ⲉϩⲟⲩⲛ ⲉⲣⲟ[ⲓ̈ ⲉϥ]
13	ⲉⲓ̈ ⲉⲕⲛⲁⲟⲩⲟⲛϩ̄ⲕ	45	ϩⲏⲛ ⲉϩⲟⲩⲛ ⲉ[ⲡⲕ]ⲱ
14	ⲉⲣⲟⲛ· ⲙ̄ⲡ̄ⲣ̄ⲟⲩⲟ	46	ϩ̄ⲧ̄· ⲡⲉⲧⲟⲩⲏⲩ ⲉ
15	ⲛ̄ϩ̄ⲕ ⲉⲣⲟⲛ ϩ̄ⲙ ⲡⲉⲕ	47	ⲃⲟⲗ ⲙ̄ⲙⲟⲓ̈ ⲉϥⲟⲩ
16	ⲉⲟⲟⲩ ⲧⲏⲣ̄ϥ̄· ⲁⲗⲗⲁ	48	ⲏⲩ ⲉⲃⲟⲗ ⲙ̄ⲡⲱⲛϩ̄:
17	ⲡⲱⲱⲛⲉ ⲙ̄ⲡⲉⲕ᾽ⲉ	49	ⲧ[ⲉ]ⲛⲟⲩ ϭⲉ ⲥⲱⲟⲩϩ
18	ⲟⲟⲩ ⲉⲕ[ⲉ]ⲉⲟⲟⲩ· ϫⲉ	50	[ⲉ]ⲣⲟⲓ̈ ⲱ̂ ⲛⲁⲙⲉⲗⲟⲥ
19	ⲕⲁⲥ᾽ ⲉⲛⲉϣϥⲓ ϩⲁ	51	[ⲉ]ⲧⲟⲩⲁⲁⲃ· ϫⲉ [. .]ⲩ
20	ⲣⲟϥ· ⲙⲏ[ⲡⲟ]ⲧⲉ ⲛ̄	52	[.]ⲛ̄ⲧⲉⲧⲛ̄ . [
21	ⲧⲛ̄ⲛⲁⲩ ⲉ[ⲣⲟⲕ ⲛ̄]ⲧⲛ̄	53	[. .] ⲁⲁⲓ̈ [.]ⲁϥ[
22	ⲕⲁ ⲧⲟ[ⲟⲧⲛ̄ ⲉⲃⲟⲗ]	54	[. . .]ⲓ̈ ⲛ̄ϭⲓ ⲡⲥ[ⲱ]
23	ϩⲁ ⲑⲟⲧ[ⲉ	55	[ⲧⲏⲣ ⲙ̄ⲡ]ⲁⲧϥ̄[
24	ⲁϥⲟⲩ[ⲱ̄ϣ̄ⲃ̄ ⲛ̄ϭⲓ ⲡⲥⲱ]	56	. [5±]ⲉⲛ . [
25	ⲧⲏⲣ· ϫⲉ . [. . .] . .	57	[.] ⲉⲣⲟϥ· ⲡⲉϫⲁ[ϥ]
26	ⲙ̄ⲙⲱⲧ̄ⲛ̄ [. . . .]ⲟⲧⲉ	58	ⲛⲁⲛ ϫⲉ ⲁⲛⲟⲕ᾽ ⲉ[ⲓ̈ϩⲛ̄]
27	ⲧⲁⲓ̈ ⲉⲧⲉ[ⲧ]ⲛ̄ⲟ ⲛ̄ϩⲟ	59	ⲧⲉⲧⲛ̄ⲙⲏⲧⲉ ⲛ̄[ⲑⲉ]
28	ⲧⲉ ϩⲏⲧ[ⲥ̄] ϫⲉⲕⲁⲥ	60	ⲛ̄ⲛⲓϣⲏⲣⲉ ϣ[ⲏⲙ:]
29	ⲛ̄ⲧⲉⲧⲛ̄ⲛⲁⲩ· ⲛ̄ⲧⲉ	61	ⲡⲉϫⲁϥ ϫⲉ ϩⲁⲙⲏ(ⲛ)[·]
30	ⲧⲛ̄ⲡⲓⲥⲧⲉⲩⲉ· ⲁⲗ	62	ⲕⲉⲕⲟⲩⲓ̈ ⲡⲉ ⲉⲓ̈ϩⲛ̄
31	ⲗⲁ ⲙ̄ⲡⲣ̄ϫⲱϩ ⲛ̄ⲧⲟϥ	63	ⲧⲉⲧⲛ̄ⲙⲏⲧⲉ· ⲁ[ϥ]
32	ⲉⲣⲟⲓ̈ ϣⲁⲛ†ⲃⲱⲕ᾽ ⲉ	64	ⲟⲩⲱ̄ϣ̄ⲃ̄ ϫⲉ ϩⲁⲙ[ⲏⲛ]

---

19 ϣ perhaps: ⲱ; ϥ perhaps: ⲛ, ⲏ.   **50–51** ⲙⲉⲗⲟⲥ GSav 9H. 4–5; GSav 100.3–5.

107

1   **12** [   ] see them.
2   2Therefore [do not be disturbed]
3   if [you (pl.)] see
4   [me.]" 3We said to him,
5   "O Lord, in what
6   form will you (sg.) reveal
7   yourself to us,
8   or (ἤ) in what kind of body
    (σῶμα)
9   will you (sg.) come? Tell us."
10   4John replied.
11   He said,
12   "Oh Lord, when you (sg.)
13   come to reveal yourself
14   to us, do not reveal
15   yourself to us in all
16   your (sg.) glory, but (ἀλλά)
17   change your glory
18   into [another] glory in order
19   that [we] may be able to bear
20   it, [lest μήποτε)]
21   we see [you (sg.) and]
22   [despair]

23   from fear [
24   5And the savior (σωτηρ)
25   [replied] that [
26   to you (pl.) this [
27   before which [you (pl.)] are
    afraid,
28   in order that
29   you (pl.) might see and
30   believe (πιστευειν).
31   6But (ἀλλά), indeed, do not
    touch
32   me, until I go

33   up to [my Father] who
34   [is] your (pl.) [Father],
35   and [my God, who]
36   is your (pl.) God,
37   and my Lord, who
38   is your (pl.) Lord.
39   7And (δέ) if
40   one is [near]

41   to me, he will [burn.]
42   8I am the [fire]
43   [that] blazes; 9who [is near]
44   [to me, is]
45   near to [the fire];
46   who is far
47   from me, is far
48   from life.
49   10Now then, gather
50   to me, O (ὦ) my holy
51   members (μέλος), for [
52   you (pl.) [
53   [
54   **13** [   ] namely the savior
    (σωτήρ)
55   [before] he
56   [
57   [ ] to him. 2[He said]
58   to us, "As for me, I [am in]
59   your (pl.) midst [as]

60   a child."
61   3He said, "Amen.
62   A little longer I am in
63   your (pl.) midst." 4[He]

64   replied, "Amen.

5–23 Cf. SophJesChr NHC III,4:91,10–20, par. **8–9** Cf. 1 Cor 15:35–44. **14–18** Cf. GPhil NHC II,3:57,28–58,10; Phil 3:21. **28–30** Cf. John 20:27–29. **31–32** Cf. John 20:17. **33–38** John 20:17. **42–43** Cf. ThomCont NHC II,7:139,39 and 140,20–30. **43–48** GThom 10 (NHC II,2:47,17–19). For the variant "life" for "kingdom" see G. Eagen, *Saint Ephrem. An Exposition of the Gospel*, 6.62. **57** Or: "to it." **58–60** ApocPaul NHC V,2:18,3–22. **59–60** Lit.: "as the little children." See H. J. Polotsky, *Collected Papers* (Jerusalem: Magnes, 1971) 230, para. 202, note 4; and Wolf-Peter Funk, "Bemerkung zum Sprachvergleich Griechisch-Koptisch," pp. 147–80 in Peter Nagel, ed., *Graeco-Coptica Griechen und Kopten im byzantinischen Ägypten* (Halle-Wittenberg: Martin-Luther-Universität, 1984), 161, note 32.

1	[. .] . ⲡⲱ[ⲟ]ⲝⲛⲉ ⲉⲣⲟ̈ⲓ	33	ⲧⲛ̄ ϩⲁⲙⲏⲛ[:
2	[. . . .] . [. .]ⲟⲩⲱ ⲱ	34	ⲟⲩ ⲱ̂ ⲣⲱ[6±] ⲙ̄
3	[6±] . ⲙⲟⲥ ⲛ̄	35	ⲙⲱⲧⲛ̄ . [. . .] . . . ⳁ
4	ⲥⲱ̈ⲓ ⲝⲉ ⲁⲛⲅ ⲟⲩⲱⲙ	36	ⲟⲩⲱⲱ ⲉⲝⲱ ⲛⲏⲧⲛ̄
5	ⲙⲟ ⲉⲣⲟϥ· ⲉⲓⲥ ϩⲏ	37	ⲙ̄ⲡⲣⲁⲱⲉ [ⲉ]ⲝⲙ̄ ⲡⲕⲟ
6	ⲛⲧⲉ ⳿ⲑⲉ ⲧⲉⲛⲟⲩ ⳁ	38	ⲥⲙⲟⲥ· ⲁ . . . . .
7	[ⲗ]ⲩⲡⲏ ⲉⲧⲃⲉ ⲛ̄ⲛⲟ	39	ⲡⲓ ⲛ̄ⲧⲟϥ ⲉⲧⲃⲉ [ⲡⲕⲟ]
8	[ⲃⲉ] ⲙ̄ⲡⲕⲟⲥⲙⲟⲥ·	40	ⲥⲙⲟⲥ ϩⲱⲥ ⲣⲱ ⲉ[ⲙ]
9	[ⲁⲗ]ⲗⲁ [⳿ⲧⲣ]ⲁⲱⲉ ⲉⲧⲃⲉ	41	ⲡⲉⲧⲛ̄ⲃⲱⲕ ⲉϩⲟ[ⲩⲛ]
10	[ⲑⲏⲩⲧ]ⲛ̄ ⲝⲉ ⲁⲧⲉⲧⲛ̄	42	ⲉⲣⲟϥ ϩⲁⲙⲏⲛ· [ⲙ̄]
11	[ⲱⲥⲕ] ⲕⲁⲗⲱⲥ ϩⲙ̄	43	ⲡ̄ⲣⲣⲓⲙⲉ ⲝⲓⲛ ⲧⲉⲛⲟⲩ
12	[ⲡⲕⲟⲥ]ⲙⲟⲥ· ⲥⲟⲩ	44	ⲁⲗⲗⲁ ⲣⲁⲱⲉ ⲛ̄ⲧⲟϥ·
13	ⲧ[. .]ⲧⲛ ⳿ⲑⲉ ⲝⲉⲕⲁⲥ	45	ϩⲁⲙⲏⲛ· ⲁ̈ⲓ̈ⲝⲣⲟ
14	ⲉⲧⲉⲧⲛⲉⳁϩⲏⲩ ⲙ̄	46	ⲉⲡⲕⲟⲥⲙⲟⲥ ⲛⲧⲱ
15	ⲙⲟ̈ⲓ ⲁⲩⲱ ⲧⲁⲣⲁ	47	ⲧⲛ̄ ⲇⲉ ⲙ̄ⲡ̄ⲣⲧⲣⲉ
16	ⲱⲉ ⲉⲝⲙ̄ ⲡⲉⲧⲛ̄ϩⲱⲃ:	48	ⲡⲕⲟⲥⲙⲟⲥ ⲝⲣⲟ ⲉ
17	ⲁⲛⲟⲕ ⲡⲉ ⲡⲣⲣⲟ [ϩ]ⲁ	49	ⲣⲱⲧⲛ̄ ϩⲁⲙⲏⲛ· ⲁ̈ⲓ
18	ⲙⲏⲛ· ⲁⲛⲟⲕ [ⲡ]ⲉ̣	50	ⲣ̄ⲣⲙ̄ϩⲉ ϩⲙ̄ ⲡⲕⲟⲥⲙⲟⲥ
19	ⲡ[ⲱⲏ]ⲣⲉ ⲙ̄ⲡ̄ⲣⲣⲟ ϩ	51	ⲛ̄ⲧ[ⲱⲧ]ⲛ̄ ϩⲱⲧⲧⲏⲩ
20	[ⲁⲙⲏⲛ·] ⲁⲛⲟⲕ ⲡ[ⲉ]	52	ⲧⲛ̄ [ⲉⲣⲡ̄]ⲙ̄ϩⲉ ⲉⲃⲟⲗ
21	[. . .] . ⲙ̄ⲙⲟ[	53	ⲙ̄[ⲙⲟϥ ϩ]ⲁⲙⲏⲛ:—
22	[. .]ⲥⲟⲩ . . [	54	[. . . . ⲛ]ⲁⲧⲥⲟ̈ⲓ ⲛ̄
23	[. .] . ˙ . [	55	[5±] . ⲟⲩⲗⲟ
24	[. .] . ⲕ . [. . .] . [	56	[6±]ⲛ ⲇⲉ ⲝⲓ
25	ⲁⲩⲱ ⲙⲛ̄ⲧⲉⲧⲛ̄[	57	[.] . [. . .]ⲱⲛ̄ϩ ⲙⲛ̄
26	[ϩⲁ]ⲙⲏⲛ· ⳁⲙⲓⲱⲉ	58	ⲡⲉⲙ̄[ⲧⲟ]ⲛ ϩⲁⲙⲏ(ⲛ)·
27	[ⲉⲝ]ⲛ̄ ⲑⲏⲩⲧⲛ̄· ⲛ̄ⲧⲱ	59	ⲥⲉⲛⲁⲕ[ⲟⲛ]ⲥ̄ⲧ ⲛ̄ⲟⲩ
28	[ⲧⲛ̄ ϩ]ⲱⲧⲧⲏⲩⲧⲛ̄	60	ⲗⲟⲅⲭⲏ [ⲙ̄ⲡ]ⲁⲥⲡⲓⲣ·
29	ⲁⲣⲓⲡⲟⲗⲉⲙⲟⲥ ϩⲁ	61	ⲡⲉⲛⲧⲁϥⲛⲁⲩ· ⲙⲁ
30	ⲙⲏⲛ· ⲥⲉⲝⲟⲟⲩ	62	ⲣⲉϥⲣ̄ⲙⲛ̄ⲧⲣⲉ· ⲁⲩ
31	[ⲙ̄]ⲙⲟ̈ⲓ ⲁⲛⲟⲕ ϩⲱⳁ	63	ⲱ ⲟⲩⲙⲉ’ ⲧⲉ ⲧⲉϥ
32	[ⲟ]ⲩⲱⲱ ⲉⲝⲉϥ ⲑⲏⲩ	64	ⲙⲛ̄ⲧⲙⲛ̄ⲧⲣⲉ ϩⲁⲙⲏ(ⲛ)·

10 At the end of the line, ⲧ appears squeezed between ⲉ and ⲛ. **43** ⲛ² ink above the letter. **52** Ink following ⲉⲃⲟⲗ appears to be splattering.

108

1	[ ] the plan against me
2–3	[
4	[after me] for I am a stranger
5	to him. 5Therefore
6	now, behold, I
7	suffer (λυπεῖν) because of the
8	[sins] of the world (κόσμος).
9	6[But (ἀλλά)] I rejoice over
10	[you (pl.)] for [you (pl.)]
11	[have continued] well (καλῶς) in
12	[the] world. [7
13	[ ] therefore in order that
14	you (pl.) may be profitable to
15	me, and I will rejoice
16	over your (pl.) work.
17	8I am the king. Amen.
18	I [am]
19	the [son] of the king.
20	[Amen.] I [am]
21–24	[
25	9And you (pl.) did not have [
26	Amen. 10I contend
27	[for] you (pl.); you (pl.)
28	too
29	take up the fight (πόλεμος).
30	Amen. 11I am
31	sent; I also
32	wish to send you (pl.).

33	Amen[12
34	[ ] O (ὦ) [
35	to you (pl.) [ ] I
36	wish to announce to you (pl.)
37	joy for the
38	world (κόσμος), but [ ]
39	concerning [the]
40	world (κόσμος), since (ὡς) indeed
41	you (pl.) [have not] entered
42	it. Amen. 13 Do
43	not weep from [now on],
44	but (ἀλλά) rather rejoice.
45	Amen. 14I have overcome
46	the world (κόσμος),
47	do not then (δέ) let
48	the world (κόσμος) overcome
49	you (pl.). Amen. 15I have
50	become free from the world (κόσμος);
51	you (pl.) too
52	[become free] from
53	[it.] Amen.
54	[16 will give] me to drink
55	[
56	[ ] and (δέ) [
57	[ ] life and
58	[rest.] Amen.
59	17I will be pierced with a
60	lance (λογχή) [in my] side.
61	18He who saw, let
62	him bear witness. And
63	true is his
64	witness. Amen.

1 Cf. Mark 3:6, par.   5 Or: "it" (masc.).   6–8 Cf. 1 Pet 3:18.   14–15 Or: "you may gain me," i.e., "may win me over"; cf. Matt 18:15: Horner reads ϯϩⲏⲩ ⲘⲠⲉⲕⲤⲞⲚ.   17 Did 14:3; Strasbourg Coptic papyrus 5 (recto).   29 But, cf. John 18:36.   30–32 John 20:21; 17:18.   42 "it," i.e., joy; cf. Matt 25:21, 23; or perhaps: "world."   45–46 John 16:33; Strasbourg Coptic papyrus 5 (verso). 49–52 Cf. John 8:36.   54 Cf. Matt 27:48, par.   59–60 John 19:34.   61–64 John 19:35; 21:24.

[P̄ΙΓ]

1   ЄΒΟΛ 2Ν̄ Μ̄ΠΗΥЄ

2   ΤΗΡΟΥ: ΤΟΤЄ Λ

3   ΝΟΝ ΝΑΠΟΣΤΟΛΟΣ

4   ΑΠЄΪΚΟΣΜΟΣ ϢϢ

5   ΠЄ Ν̄ΘЄ Ν̄ΝΙΚΑΚЄ

6   Ν[Ν]Α2ΡΑΝ· ΑΝΡΘЄ

7   [Ν̄Ν]ЄΤ2Ν̄ ΝΑΙϢΝ

8   [Μ̄ΠЄ]ΟΟΥ· ЄΡЄΝЄ(Ν)

9   . [. . .]ϢΤЄ Ν̄ΜΠΗ

10 Ο[ΥЄ Τ]Η[Ρ]ΟΥ[·]ЄΡЄ

11 Τ[. . .] . †[Ν̄ΤЄ]ΝΜΝ̄Τ

12 Α[Π]ΟΣΤΟΛΟΣ 2ΙϢ

13 [Ϣ]Ν· ΑΥϢ ΑΝΝΑΥ

14 [Є]ΠЄΝΣϢΤΗΡ Ν̄

15 [Τ]ЄΡЄϤΠϢ2 ЄΤΜЄ

16 [2]ϤΤΟЄ Μ̄ΠЄ· Α[

17 [7±   ]ЄϤ . [

18 [

19 [. . .] . [

20 [. . .] . Ν . [

21 [. .]Є . [

22 [. . .]Ν̄[

23 Χ . ΑΜ[. . .]ϢΤ̄[Ρ̄]

24 Τ̄Ρ̄· Α[ΝΑ]ΓΓЄΛΟΣ

25 Μ̄Ν ΝΑΡΧΗΑΓΓЄ

26 ΛΟΣ ΠϢΤ ЄΥЄΧ̄Μ̄

27 Π[·]Υ2[. . . Ν]ЄΧЄ

28 ΡΟ[Υ]ΒΪ[Μ

29 2Α ΠЄ . [

30 ΜЄ Α[

31 ΚΑΝ ЄΥΤ[Μ̄ЄΙ ЄΠЄ]

32 ΣΗΤ· ΑΝ . . . [

33 ЄΤΜ[

34 ΤΑΠЄ[

35 2ΥΜ . [

36 ΣΒ . . Є . [

37 ΟΣ 2ΙΝЄ . [

38 ΑΥΝΟΥΧЄ [Ν̄ΝЄΥ]

39 ΚΛΟΜ' ЄΠ[ЄΣΗΤ]

40 2ΙΘΗ Μ̄ΠЄ[ΘΡΟΝΟΣ]

41 Μ̄ΠΙϢΤ· Α[ΝЄΤΟΥ]

42 ΑΑΒ ΤΗΡ[ΟΥ ΧΙ ΝЄΥ]

43 ΣΤΟΛΗ[

44 ΝΤЄΡЄ[

45 ϢΗΡ[Є

46 Є . [

47–52 [

53 . . . · ЄΤΒ[Є ΟΥ]

54 ΚΡΙΜЄ· ΑΥ[Ϣ ЄΚΜΟ]

55 Κ̄2 Ν̄2ΗΤ Ν̄Τ[ΟΚ]

56 2ϢΣΤЄ Ν̄ΤЄ[ΤΑΓ]

57 ΓЄΛΙΚΗ Τ[Η]Ρ̄Σ̄ [ϢΤ̄Ρ̄]

58 Τ̄Ρ̄ Ν̄[Τ]ΑϤΟΥϢ[ϢΒ]

59 [Ν̄ΤЄΪ]2Є· ΧЄ[

60 [5±   ] . ΝЄΠ[

61 [5±   ] . ΝΧ[.]Є [

62 [5±   ] . . Ο[.] . [

63 [. . . .] ΑΝ[

64 [. . .] ΑΚΧ . [

---

27 Or: "ΧЄΡΟ[Υ]ΒΪ[Ν ." **35** Perhaps: 2ΥΜΝ[ΟΣ or 2ΥΜΝ[ЄΥЄ; see frg. 9F.7. **35/36** Perhaps: ΠΡЄ]/ΣΒΥΤЄΡ[ΟΣ.

[113]

1   **14** from all the
2   heavens. ²Then (τότε),
3   as for us apostles (ἀπόστολος),
4   this world (κόσμος) became
5   as the darkness
6   [before] us. ³We became as
7   [those] among the Aeons (αἰών)
8   [of glory]. ⁴Our

9   [   ] of [all]
10   the heavens, as

11   [   ] invested us
12   with [our] apostleship
     (ἀπόστολος).
13   ⁵And we saw
14   our savior (σωτήρ),
15   [after] he attained to the
16   [fourth] heaven. [
17–22 [

23   [   ] disturbance.
24   ⁶[The] angels (ἄγγελος)
25   and the archangels
     (ἀρχηάγγελος)
26   [fled. They are] over
27   the [7   the]
28   Cherubim (χερουβίμ) [
29   under the [
30   [
31   even though (κἄν) they [do not
     descend]
32   [

38   ⁸they cast [their]
39   crowns [down]
40   at the front of the [throne
     (θρόνος)]
41   of the Father.
42   ⁹All [the holy ones received
     their]
43   robes (στολή) [¹⁰
44   after [

45   son [
46–52 [

53   [¹¹   why]
54   are you (sg.) weeping and
55   [distressed]
56   so that (ὥστε) the entire
57   angelic (ἀγγελικός) (host) [is
     disturbed]?
58   ¹²He replied
59   [in this] manner that [
60–64 [

5 Lit.: "darknesses"; see note on p. 107.59–60.   **11–12** Strasbourg Coptic papyrus 6 (verso): p. 158.   **14–16** In The Gospel of Mary, the soul attains rest after overcoming the fourth power; 16,21–17,7.   **38–41** Cf. Rev 4:10.   **42** Perhaps: "saints."   **42–43** Cf. Rev 6:11.

[Pׁ]

1   [6±   ]ос епеї
2   [6±   ]а еїмо
3   [кׁ2 N̄2HT е]мате
4   [6±   ]моуоут
5   [5±   ] 2ITм̄ пла
6   [ос м̄]пїн̄λ· ⲱ па
7   [еіⲱт] еⲱⲭе оун
8   [ⲱбом] марепеїа
9   [пот с]аат· мароу
10 [5±   ]˙ 2ITN̄ ке
11 [6±   ]. N̄реqⲣ̄
12 [7±   ]е еуⲱa(N)
13 [7±   ]. ⲓ̄ⲏ̄λ
14 [   ]. а
15–20 [

21 [5±   ]. поуⲭаі
22 [. . . . ⲱ]ⲱпе м̄пко
23 [см]ос тⲏⲣq̄: —
24 [е]іе оn апⲱⲏре
25 [п]а2тq еxⲛ̄ м̄пат
26 [е]пеqїⲱт [е]qⲭⲱ
27 [м̄]мос· ⲭ[е ⲱ паеі]
28 [ⲱ]т· мⲏ[
29 [.]т. м̄.[
30 [.].[.]по[
31 [. . . .]пм[
32 [. . . .]т†с[б̄тⲱт]

33 емоу 2N̄ оураⲱе
34 ауⲱ тапⲱ2т е
35 вол м̄пасноq е
36 x̄м̄ пгенос N̄N
37 рⲱме· алла еї
38 ріме м̄мат[е е]т
39 ве намера[те] е
40 те наі не а[ⲃра2а]м
41 мⲛ̄ їсаак [мⲛ̄ ї]а
42 кⲱв· ⲭе е[уна]ⲱ
43 а2ера[то]у [м̄п]е
44 2ооу м̄п2ап[е]ї
45 на2мо[о]с 2іп[а]
46 ⲑроnoc та† 2[ап]
47 епкосмос с[ена]
48 ⲭоос наї ⲭе е[
49 [. .]а⊝ⲏ .[
50 [
51 [   ] . . [
52 [   ]аⲭ.[
53 [N]аї .[
54 [   ]а . [ ].
55 . к [. . . .]. т. на
56 сⲱ . .[. етве пе
57 ооу N̄таутааq
58 наї 2іx̄м̄ [п]ка2·
59 ⲱ па[їⲱт е]ⲱ[ⲱп]е
60 [оунⲱбо]м [ма]ре
61 [пеїапот] саат:
62 [7±   ]наq м̄
63 [пме2с]еп снау
64 [. . .] . . ⲱⲏре N̄ⲅ

4 Cf. frg. 25F.4.   **40** аⲃра2ам is the expected locution, but is too long for the lacuna. The restoration assumes that 2а or ⲣа has been written over the line, as occurs with о at p. 97.29, or that the entire word is crowded in as occurs regularly at ends of lines in this text.   **59** ⲱ is perhaps: ⲱ.

[114]

1   [13   ] to this
2   [   ] I am
3   greatly [distressed]
4   [   ] kill
5   [   ] upon the people
    (λαός)
6   [of] Israel. 14O (ὦ) my
7   [Father], if
8   [it is possible], let this
9   [cup] pass by me. 15Let them
10 [   ] by another
11 [   ] those who do
12 [   ] if they
13 [   ] Israel
14–20 [

21 [16   ] salvation
22 [   ] come to the entire
23 [world (κόσμος)].
24 17[Then] again the son
25 bowed his knees
26 [to] his Father, saying
27 ["O (ὦ) my Father]
28–31 [

32 [18   I am ready]

33 to die with joy
34 and pour out
35 my blood upon
36 the human race (γένος).
37 19Yet (ἀλλά) I

38 weep only
39 for my [beloved],
40 who are [Abraham]
41 and Isaac [and Jacob],
42 that [they may be able]
43 to stand [in the]
44 day of judgment[.] 20I
45 will sit upon [my]
46 throne (θρόνος), and I will
    [judge]
47 the world (κόσμος). 21[They
    will]
48 say to me that [
49–52 [
53 [22   to] me [
54 [
55 [   ] shall
56 [because of] the
57 glory [that] was given
58 to me upon [the] earth.
59 23O (ὦ) my [Father, if]
60 [it is possible, let]
61 [this cup] pass by me.
62 [24   ] for
63 [the] second time
64 [   ] son, and you (sg.)

6–9 Matt 26:39; cf. lines 59–61. 24–26 Matt 26:42; Mark 14:39.
34–37 Mark 14:24; Matt 26:28; Luke 22:20. 36–37 "human race" perhaps: "race
of men." 38–44 Cf. Rom 11:25–32. 41 Cf. GSav frg. 9H.6: αΒΡΑ[2ΑΜ? 44–47
Matt 25:31–33. 47–48 Matt 25:37, 44 (?). 56–58 John 7:39; 11:4; 12:16, 23,
28; 13:31–32; 14:13; 15:8; 17:4–5. 59–61 Cf. lines 6–9.

115*

1–21	[
22	. [
23	ⲣ[
24	ⲉ[
25	ⲛ[
26	ⲟ[
27	ⲛⲁ . [
28	ⲛϥ[
29	ⲁⲡϣⲏⲣⲉ ⲟ[
30	ⲙⲡⲙⲉϩϣⲟ[ⲙⲛⲧ]
31	ⲛ̄ⲥⲟⲡ· ϫⲉ ⲱ̣ [ⲡⲁⲓ̈]
32	ⲱⲧ' ⲉϣϫⲉ ⲡ[

116*

1–19	[	
20	[	] .
21	[	
22	[	] .
23	[	]ⲉ
24	[	]ⲙ
25	[	]ⲧ̣·
26	[	]ⲥ
27	[	] ⲙ̄ⲛ
28	[	] ⲟ̣ⲥ
29	[2-3]ⲱ̣ⲗ . ⲣ̣· ⲁϥ	
30	[2-3]ⲭⲱⲕ ⲉⲃⲟⲗ ⲛ̄	
31	[ⲧⲗⲉ]ⲓ̣ⲧⲟⲩⲣⲅⲓⲁ ϣⲁ(ⲛ)	
32	[ⲧ⸗. ⲃ]ⲱⲕ ϣⲁⲣⲟⲟⲩ·	

115/116 Fragment 4F/H is a sheet. Its relationship to the preceding numbered pages is unknown. The pages of 4F/H have been designated 115*, 116*, 121*, 122* for convenience in referencing. The precise relationship of frgs. 4–30 to pages 97–114 is unknown.   116. 29 ⲣ perhaps: ⲩ.

115*

1–28 [

29   the son [

30   the third

31   time: "O (ῶ) [my]

32   [Father] if [

116*

1–28

29   [   ] He

30   [   ] complete

31   [the] service (λειτουργία) until

32   [   ] go to them.

115.29–32 Cf. Matt 26:42–44.   116.31 Cf. Luke 1:23.

121*

1	[6±] . ⲉⲃⲟⲗ		33	ⲉⲡⲱ[ⲧⲛ
2	[6±]ⲧⲏⲣⲟⲩ		34	ⲧⲛ[
3	[7±] ⲙ̄ⲡⲧ .		35	ⲁⲩⲛ[
4	[9±]ϥ̄ ⲁ		36	ⲛ̄ⲧⲟ[
5	[9±] . ⲛ:		37	ⲛ̄ⲁ . [
6	[9±] . .		38	. [
7–19	[		39–58	[
20	ⲉ . [			
21	ⲉ . [			
22	ⲉ . [			
23	ⲟⲩ[			
24	. . [			
25	. [			
26	ⲟⲩ[			
27	ⲧⲣ[. .] . [		59	. [
28	ⲡⲣⲟⲫⲏⲧⲏⲥ [. . ⲡⲉ]		60	[
29	ϫⲁϥ ⲛⲁⲛ ⲛ̄ϭ[. .] . .		61	[.] . ⲉ ⲙ[
30	ϫⲉ ⲙ̄ⲛ ⲕⲗⲏⲣ[ⲟⲥ ⲟ]ⲩ		62	ⲡϣⲉ ⲙ̄[
31	ⲟⲧⲃ̄ ⲉⲡⲱⲧⲛ̄· ⲟⲩ[ⲧⲉ]		63	ⲡϣⲙ[
32	ⲙ̄ⲛ ⲉⲟⲟⲩ ⲉϥϫⲟⲥ[ⲉ]		64	ⲡϣⲉⲣ[

Top margin visible; double columns.   **1–6** Frg. 8H.   **5** Perhaps: ⲉⲁⲙ]ⲏⲛ:.   **33–38** Frg. 8H.   **64** ⲣ perhaps: ⲩ.

121*

1	[
2	[ ] all
3–26	[
27	[
28	prophet ($\pi\rho o\phi\acute{\eta}\tau\eta s$) [ ] said
29	to us [ ]
30	that no [lot ($\kappa\lambda\hat{\eta}\rho os$)] surpasses
31	your (pl.) own. [And ($o\mathring{\upsilon}\tau\epsilon$)]
32	there is no glory that is more
	exalted

33	than [your own
34–60	[
61	[
62	the wood [of
63–64	[

122*

1	[. . ⲦⲘⲚ]ⲧⲭⲱⲱⲣⲉ·	33	ⲣϥ̄ ⲛ̄ⲛⲁ[
2	[6±]ⲃⲉ ⲉⲃⲟⲗ·	34	ⲛ̄ⲁⲅⲁⲑ[ⲟⲛ
3	[. . . . ⲘⲚ]ⲧⲉⲣⲟ	35	ⲱ̄ ⲡⲉ[ⲥ̄ⲣ̄ⲟⲥ̄
4	[5± Ⲙ]ⲏⲧⲓ Ⲙ̄	36	ⲱ[
5	[7±]ⲧⲣⲟ	37	ⲧ . [
6	[9±]ⲩ	38	. . [
7–25	[	39–51	[
		52	[10±] . ⲁ
		53	[9±] . ⲁⲓ̈
		54	[7±]ⲥ ϥⲟ̄ⲥ̄
		55	[10±] . .
		56	[11±] .
		57	[11±] .
		58	[9±] . ⲏⲩ
		59	[7±]ϩ[.] . ⲁ
		60	[. . ⲛ̄ϣ]ⲟⲙⲛ̄ⲧ ⲛ̄ϩⲟ
		61	ⲟ[ⲩ ⲧⲁ]ϫⲓ ⲑⲏⲩⲧ̄ⲛ̄
26	[ ] .	62	ⲉ[ⲧⲡ]ⲉ ⲛ̄ⲙⲙⲁⲓ̈· ⲧⲁ
27	[ ] .	63	[ⲧ]ⲥⲁⲃⲉ ⲑⲏⲩⲧ̄ⲛ̄ ⲉ
28	[	64	[ⲣ]ⲉⲧⲉⲧⲛ̄ⲉⲡⲓⲑⲩ
29	[ ]ⲁⲙ .		
30	[ ] . ⲁⲟ . ⲉ		
31	[ϩ]ⲁⲓ̈ⲃⲉⲥ		
32	[ ] . ⲣⲱ ⲱ̄ ⲡⲧⲏ		

Top margin visible; double columns.   **1–6** Frg. 8F.   **33–38** Frg. 8F.   **59** . perhaps:
ⲏ, ⲓ, ⲛ, ⲡ.   **64** The first line of the next page would have begun [ⲘⲒⲀ.

122*

1	[	the] strength.	33	of [	
2	[		34	good (ἀγαθός) [	
3	[	] kingdom	35	O (ὦ) [cross (σταυρός)	
4	[	] (μήτι)	36	[	
5–30	[		37–53	[	
			54	[	] cross (σταυρός)
			55–58	[	
			59	[	
			60	[in] three days,	
			61	[and I will] take you (pl.)	
			62	to [heaven] with me, and	
31	[	] shadow	63	teach you (pl.). Since	
32	[	] O (ὦ) Entirety	64	your (pl.) desire (ἐπιθυμία)	

60 Cf. Mark 8:31; 9:31; 10:34.

5F

1–18	[	33–52	[
19	[. . .] . ⲛ ⲁⲗⲗ[ⲁ ⲁ̄ⲛ̄ⲅ]		
20	[ⲟⲩⲣ̄ⲙ̄]ⲙⲁⲟ· ⲧ̄ⲛⲁ		
21	[ⲙⲁ̄ⲍ̄ⲕ ⲉⲃ]ⲟⲗ ϩ̄ⲛ ⲧⲁ	53	. [
22	[ⲙ̄ⲛ̄ⲧⲣ̄ⲙ̄]ⲙⲁⲟ· ⲕⲉ	54	ⲡⲉ[
23	ⲕⲟ[ⲩ̈] ⲡⲉ ⲱ̑ ⲡⲉⲥ̄ⲣ̄ⲟ̄ⲥ	55	ⲛ̄ⲟ . [
24	ⲛ̄ⲧⲉⲡⲉⲧϣⲁⲁⲧ	56	ⲡ[
25	ϫⲱⲕ· ⲁⲩⲱ ⲛ̄ⲧⲉ	57	[
26	ⲡⲉⲧϭⲟ.ⲭ̄ⲃ ⲙⲟⲩϩ·	58	. [
27	ⲕⲉⲕⲟⲩ̈ ⲡⲉ ⲱ̑ ⲡⲉ	59–61	[
28	ⲥ̄ⲣ̄ⲟ̄ⲥ ⲛ̄ⲧⲉⲡⲉⲛ		
29	ⲧⲁϥ[ϩⲉ] ⲧⲱⲟⲩⲛ·		
30	[ⲕⲉⲕⲟ]ⲩ̈ ⲡⲉ ⲱ̑ ⲡⲉ	62	ⲙⲁ[
31	ⲥ̄ⲣ̄ⲟ̄ⲥ ⲛ̄ⲧⲉⲡⲉⲡⲗⲏ	63	ⲡ . [
32	ⲣⲱⲙⲁ [ⲧ]ⲏⲣ̄ϥ ϫⲱⲕ	64	ⲙ[

Fragment 5F may be the bottom part of p. 106; see the Introduction.

5F

1–18	[
	33–64 [

19   [   ] but (ἀλλά) [I am]
20   rich. I will
21   [fill you (sg.)] with my
22   wealth.
23   [A little longer], O (ὦ̂) cross
         (σταυρός),
24   and that which is lacking
25   is perfected, and
26   that which is diminished is full.
27   A little longer, O (ὦ̂)
28   cross (σταυρός), and that which
29   [fell] arises.
30   A [little longer], O (ὦ̂)
31   cross (σταυρός), and all
32   the pleroma (πλήρωμα) is
         perfected.

23, 27, 30 GSav, p. 107.62.   **24, 26, 28** Or: "he who."   **24–32** Cf. TreatRes
NHC I,4:48,38–49,5.

5H

1–19	[		33–50	[	
			51	[. .] . ⲛ̄ϣⲟ[ⲣ̄ⲡ̄ . . . ⲧⲱ]	
20	[	] .	52	ⲟⲩⲛ̄ ⲉϩⲣⲁⲓ̈[. . . .]	
21	[	] . [.]	53	ⲱ̂ ⲡⲉⲥ̄ⲣ̄[ⲟ̄ⲥ	
22	[	]ⲟⲩⲛ	54	ⲙ̄ⲙⲟⲕ[	
23	[	]ⲉⲣⲟⲕ	55	ϫⲓⲥⲉ ϩⲛ̄ ⲧ . [	
24	[	ϩⲁ]ⲙⲏ(ⲛ)	56	ϫⲉ ⲡⲉⲕⲟⲩⲱϣ ⲡⲉ	
25	[		57	ⲡⲁⲓ̈· ⲱ̂ ⲡⲉⲥ̄ⲣ̄ⲟ̄ⲥ·	
26	[	]ⲕ	58	ⲙ̄ⲡⲣ̄ⲣ̄ϩⲟⲧⲉ ⲁⲛⲅ	
27–28	[		59	ⲟⲩⲣ̄ⲙⲙⲁⲟ ϯⲛⲁ	
			60	ⲙⲁϩⲕ ⲉⲃⲟⲗ ϩ̄ⲛ ⲧⲁ	
29	[	] . .	61	ⲙⲛ̄ⲧⲣ̄ⲙ̄[ⲙⲁⲟ·]ϯ	
30	[	]ⲧ	62	ⲛⲁⲧⲁⲗⲉ ⲉ[ϩⲣⲁⲓ̈ ⲉ]	
31	[	] . ϩⲟⲩ	63	ϫⲱⲕ ⲱ̂ ⲡⲉⲥ̄ⲣ̄ⲟ̄ⲥ	
32	[	]ⲟⲩ	64	ⲥⲉⲛⲁⲁϣ[ⲁⲓ̈] ⲉⲣⲟⲕ	

Fragment 5H may be the bottom part of p. 105; see the Introduction.
58–61 Cf. GSav 5F.19–22.

5H

1–22 [

23   [   ] to you (sg.)
24   [Amen]
25–32 [

33–50 [
51   [   ] first [
52   rise up [
53   O (ὦ) cross (σταυρός) [
54   to you (sg.) [
55   exalted among [
56   for this [is] your (sg.)
57   desire, O (ὦ) cross (σταυρός).
58   Do not be afraid; I am
59   rich. I will
60   fill you (sg.) with my
61   wealth[.] I
62   will mount
63   you, O (ὦ) cross (σταυρός).
64   They will [be more numerous]
        than you (sg.)

51–52 Cf. 1 Thess 4:16 (?).

6F

1   [   ]ⲓ̄ ⲙⲡⲉ[
2   [   ] . . [

6H

1   [   ]ϩⲓⲭ̅ⲙ̣[

7F

1   [   ] . ϯⲣⲉ
2   [   ]ⲛ· ϣⲟ
3   [   ] . ⲡⲉⲥ̣[ⲣ̅ⲟ̅ⲥ]
4   [   ] . ⲁ̅ⲡ̅ [
5   [ ] . . [

33   ⲉ̣[
34–37 [

7H

1   [   ] .
2–5 [

33   ⲟⲓⲕⲟ[
34   ⲧⲉⲧ . [
35   [.] . ⲛⲛϣ̣[
36   [. . ⲥ̅]ⲣ̣ⲟ̅[ⲥ̅
37   [. . . .]ⲉ̣ . [

6F Top margin visible.   **6H** Top margin visible.   **7F** Top margin visible; double columns.   **7H** Top margin visible; double columns.

6F

1–2   [

6H

1   [   ] upon [
2   [

7F

1–2   [33–37 [
3   [cross (σταυρός)
4–5   [

7H

1–5   [33–35 [
                                      36   [   ] cross (σταυρός)[
                                      37   [

9F

1	[	]ce	33	. [	
2	[	]ро оуа	34	cenaϣ . [. .] . .	
3	[	]ñтсофі	35	an ñбı ꙅenмнн[ϣe]	
4	[ⲁ	]мıc· пϣe	36	eımнтı петnⲁ[	
5	[	]птнр̄q̄	37	[ ]упос м̄м[	
6	[	eв]оⲗ ñne	38	[ ]vacat ñтереq . [	
7	[	]ϣоу·	39	[ ]ꙅумнеуe[	
			40	[ ] . . [.]ï[	

9H

1	[ ] .	33	[.]n[	
2	[ ]c . [. .] . cм̄ñтq̄	34	м̄ñ n̄[.]ϣ[м̄ñ]	
3	[e]рon · пеxaq nⲁ(n)	35	ñcⲱc м[	
4	[x]e ⲱ̄ nⲁмeⲗoc eт	36	xнc м̄п[5± про]	
5	оуⲁⲁв· nⲁ[ïⲁт тн]у	37	фнтн[c	
6	[т]ñ̄ xe aпⲁï ⲱ[	38	aврⲁ[	
7	[.]e тнутñ̄[	39	aⲕ . [	
8	[. .] . [.]x . [			

9F Top margin is not visible. Double columns.   **2** Perhaps: xe]ро or e]рооу ⲁ.
40 . [1] perhaps: †, ф, ꝑ.   **9H** Top margin is not visible. Double columns.   **2** . [2] perhaps tail of: q, ꝑ, †.   **8** . [2] perhaps: ꙅ, в.   **38** Perhaps: aврⲁ[ꙅⲁм.   **39** Perhaps: ıcⲁ]/aⲕ.   Note: Frg. 8F/H is placed at the top of pp. 121/122.

9F

1–2	[
3	[ ] of the wisdom (σοφία)
4	[ ]. The wood
5	[ ] all
6	[ ] from the [
7	[

33	[
34	they will [
35	[ ] namely multitudes [
36	except (εἰ μήτι) the one who will [
37	[
38	[ ] after he [
39	[ ] sing (ὑμνεύειν)[
40	[

9H

1	[
2	[ ] establish it
3	[among] us? He said to us,
4	"O (ὦ) my holy
5	members (μέλος), [blessed are you (pl.)],
6	for this one has [
7	you (pl.) [
8	[

33	[
34	and [
35	after [
36	[
37	[prophet (προφήτης)
38–39	[

9F.39 Mark 14:26; Matt 26:30; cf. Rev 4:10.   **9H.4–5** P. 100.3–5; p. 107.50–51.

10F

1	[	] .		33	ϩⲁⲙ[ⲏⲛ
2	[	] ·		34	ⲓ̈ⲁⲕⲱⲃ[
3	[	] . ⲉⲁⲩ		35	ⲥⲏⲥ ⲡⲡ[
4	[	]ⲉⲣⲟⲕ		36	ⲛ̄ϣⲁ . [
5	[	] ⲕ·		37	ⲛ̄ⲧⲉ[
6	[			38	ⲁ . [

10H

1	[	]ⲁⲗⲗⲱⲥ		33	[
2	[	ⲥ] . . ⲧⲥⲟ		34	. [
3	[	ⲉⲃ]ⲟⲗ ⲛ̄ⲧⲉϥ		35	ⲧⲥ[
4	[	]ⲙ' ⲉⲧ		36	ⲧⲉⲛ[
5	[	]ⲛ' ⲁϥ		37	ⲣ ⲉⲃⲟ[ⲗ
6	[	]‾. .		38	[

11F

29	[	] . . [
30	[	ⲱ̄ ⲡ]ⲉⲥ ⲣ̄ⲟ̄[ⲥ
31	[	ⲟ]ⲩⲏⲩ ⲉⲃⲟ[ⲗ
32	[	]ⲉϥⲟⲩⲏⲩ[

11H

29	[	] . . [ ]
30	[	ⲥ̄]ⲣ̄ⲟ̄ⲥ ϩⲁ[.] . [
31	[	]ⲧ ⲙ̄ⲡⲁⲟ[
32	[	] . ⲕ ϩⲁⲙⲏ[ⲛ

10F Top margin is not visible. Double columns.   **2** Or: ⲓ̈ⲁⲕⲱⲃ[ⲟⲥ.   **2–3** Perhaps: ⲙⲱⲩ̈]ⲥⲏⲥ.   **10H** Top margin is not visible. Double columns.   **11F** Bottom margin visible. Vestiges of letters on extended vellum are perhaps a marginal note, or part of another column, if vellum is twisted. It seems that these letters are by the same hand:

>]ⲙ̄[
>] . ⲟ[

11H Bottom margin visible.   **29** .¹ perhaps: ϯ, ⲣ, ⲫ, ϥ.   **30** .¹ most like ⲁ, not ⲏ.

10F

1–3　[

4　　[　　　　　　　] to you (sg.)
5–6　[

33　　Amen [
34　　Jacob [
35　　　[
36–38 [

10H

1　　[　　　　　　] otherwise (ἄλλως)
2　　[
3　　[　　　　] from his
4　　[
5　　[　　　　　] he
6　　[

33–38 [

11F

29　[
30　[　　O (ὦ)] cross (σταυρός) [
31　[　　　] to be far from [
32　[　　　] since he is far [

11H

29　[
30　[　　] cross (σταυρός) [
31　[
32　[　　] you (sg.). Amen [

10F.34 Or: "James."

12F

31 [   ] . [.] ЄⲂⲦ[
32 [   ] . ⲬЄ ⲚⲦЄ . [

12H

30 [   ]ЄⲚ . . [
31 [   ]ⲦⲀⲬⲢⲎⲨ[
32 [   ] vacat Є[

13F

32 [   ] ⲔⲚⲀ . [

13H

32 [   ]Єⲱⲱⲱ[

12F Bottom margin visible.   **32** .² perhaps: †, ⲣ, ⲫ, ⲯ.   **12H** Bottom margin visible.
31 Cf. Luke 16:26; Mark 16:20; Matt 7:25.   **32** Є may be carryover from line 2, or
possibly a subscript title.   **13F** Bottom margin visible.   **13H** Bottom margin visible.

12F
31–32 [

12H
30   [
31   [   ] be firm [
32   [

13F
32   [

13H
32   [

12H.31 Matt 7:25(?).

14F

18 [. . . .] . . . [
19 [.] . ⲛⲉ ⲙⲙ[
20 [.]ⲏⲥ· ⲉⲣⲉ[
21 [.]ϩⲉⲛⲟⲩⲟ[
22 [. . .] ϩⲛ ⲧⲡⲟ[ⲗⲓⲥ ⲧ]
23 [ⲉⲧⲙ]ⲙⲁⲩ· ⲁ[ⲛ.ⲝⲟⲟⲥ]
24 [ⲇⲉ ⲉⲡ]ⲥⲱⲧⲏ[ⲣ ⲭⲉ ⲁⲱ]
25 ⲧⲉ ⲧⲉïⲡⲟⲗ[ⲓⲥ ⲡⲉ]
26 ⲭⲁϥ ⲛⲁⲛ [ⲭⲉ ⲛⲧⲟⲥ]
27 ⲧⲉ ⲑⲓⲗ̅ⲏⲙ [
28 [. .]ⲡⲟⲗⲓⲥ [
29 [.] . ⲧⲉⲧⲉ[ⲛⲁ]
30 ⲙⲉⲣⲁⲧⲉ[
31 [.]ⲁϭ· ⲱⲛ̅ϩ[
32 ⲉⲛⲁⲥⲱ . [

14H

18 [   ] . . [
19 [   ]ϥⲟⲩⲟⲛ[ϩ]
20 [. . . .] . ⲙ̅ⲛ ⲗⲁⲁ[ⲩ]
21 [5± ⲉ]ⲣⲟϥ` ⲟⲩ
22 [ⲧⲉ ⲙ̅ⲛ ⲗ]ⲁⲁⲩ ⲁⲙ[ⲁϩ]
23 [ⲧⲉ ⲙ̅ⲙ]ⲟϥ ϩⲓⲧ̅ⲙ [ⲡ]
24 [. . .] . · ⲁⲛ.ⲝ[ⲛⲟⲩϥ]
25 [ⲉⲛ.ⲝ]ⲱ ⲙ̅ⲙⲟⲥ ⲭⲉ
26 [ⲁⲱ ⲡⲉ ⲡ]ⲉïⲙⲁ ⲉⲧ
27 [   ] . ⲧⲉⲧⲡⲉ .
28 [   ]ⲡⲉⲭⲁϥ[
29 [   ]ⲧⲉⲥⲕⲏ[
30 [   ]ⲱⲧ ⲭⲓⲛⲧⲁ[
31 [   ]ⲉ ⲟⲩⲱⲡ[ⲏⲣⲉ]
32 [   ]ⲧⲉ ⲉϭⲱ . [

14F Left margin and bottom margin are visible.   **18** .¹ perhaps: ⲧ, ⲣ, ⲫ, ⳓ.   **30** Cf.
p. 114.32.   **32** .¹ perhaps: ⲧ.   **14H** Right margin and bottom margin are
visible.   **29** Perhaps: ⲧⲉⲥⲕⲏ[ⲛⲏ ($\sigma\kappa\eta\nu\acute{\eta}$).

14F

18–21 [

22 [   ] in [that]

23 [city (πόλις). And (δέ) we said]

24 [to the] savior (σωτήρ): [“What]

25 is this city (πόλις)?” He

26 [said] to us: [“It]

27 is Jerusalem [

28 [   ] city (πόλις) [

29 [my]

30 beloved [

31 [   ] live [

32 [

14H

18 [

19 [   ] reveal

20 [   ] no one

21 [   ] him [nor (οὔτε)]

22 any [seize]

23 him by [the]

24 [   ] We [asked him],

25 [saying],

26 [“What is] this place, which

27 [

28 [   ] He said [

29 [

30 [   ] since [

31 [   ] a wonder [

32 [

15F

33	[	] . . .	1	[	
34	[	] . oc	2	ρ[	
35	[	] . є	3	φ[	

15H

33	[		1	. [	
34	[		2	[	
35	[	]м	3	ċ[	
36	[	]γ	4	?[	

16F

1	[	]	33	ω[	
2	[		34	. [	
3	[		35	. [	
4	[	] .	36	[	

16H

1	[	]x̣	33–35	[	
2	[	]			
3	[	] .			
4	[	]	36	. [	

15F Center fold of a sheet; two columns. Sheet folds with flesh side on the outside of folded sheet. The two columns are part of two different pages. Top and bottom margins are not visible. **15H** Center fold of a sheet; two columns. Sheet folds with hair side on the inside of folded sheet. The two columns are part of two different pages. Top and bottom margins are not visible. **16F/H** Center of a double column with ink on both sides. On the flesh side the tail of a margin decoration and ω are identifiable. On the hairside, perhaps ⲁ or x. **16F.1** Vestige of ink to the left of ω appears to be the tail of a margin decoration. **16H.1** x̣ perhaps: ⲁ̣.

15F

33–36   [1–3   [

15H

33–36   [1–4   [

16F

1–4   [33–36 [

16H

1–4   [33–36 [

17F

1   [   ] .
2   [   ]ϣH
3   [   ] . ⲁⲡⲣⲟ
4   [   ]ⲙⲟⲟⲩ
5   [   ]ⲇⲓⲕⲁⲓⲟⲥ
6   [   ] . ⲉⲣⲟⲟⲩ .
7   [   ]ⲉ . . [

17H

1   [. .] . [
2   ⲛⲅ . [
3   ⲉⲡ . [
4   ⲉⲕ2ⲙ[ⲟⲟⲥ ⲉⲧⲟⲩ]
5   ⲛⲁⲙ ⲛ̄[ⲡⲓ̈ⲱⲧ 2ⲓⲭ̄ⲙ̄]
6   ⲡⲉⲕⲑⲣ[ⲟⲛⲟⲥ
7   [. .]ⲉ . [

18F

1   [   ] . ⲛⲉ[
2   [   ] . ⲧ2ⲧ[
3   [   ] . [.] . ⲁ[

18H

1   ⲛⲥ[
2   ϭⲓⲭ[
3   ⲁⲓ̈ⲛ[

17F Right margin visible.   17H Left margin visible.   18F No margins visible.
18H Left margin visible.

17F

1–4	[
5	[ ] righteous (δίκαιος)
6	[ ] to them
7	[

17H

1–2	[
3	[
4	[sitting at the]
5	right hand [of the Father upon]
6	your (sg.) [throne (θρόνος)
7	[

18F

1–3	[

18H

1	[
2	hand [
3	I [

17H.4–6 P. 114.44–46; Cf. Mark 14:62, par.; Mark 16:19, Matt 26:64; Rom 8:34; Col 3:1; Heb 1:3; 8:1; 12:2; 1 Pet 3:22; Acts 2:34; Ps 110:1.

19F

1   [. . .] . . . [
2   пх̄ωωμε м̄п[
3   ⲛ̄ϩ· ⲛ̄ⲛⲉⲩⲣ̄пⲙ[ⲉ]
4   ⲉⲩⲉ ⲛ̄ⲧⲉϥ[ⲣⲉ]ⲛ̣[ⲉⲁ]
5   ⲉⲣⲉⲧⲉϥⲥ[ϩⲓ]ⲙⲉ̣ [ⲛⲁ]
6   ⲣ̄ⲭⲏⲣⲁ· [ⲛ̄ⲧⲉⲛⲉϥ]
7   [ϣ]ⲏⲣⲉ ϣ[ⲏⲙ ⲣ̄ⲁⲧⲉⲓ]
8   [ⲱⲧ.]ⲉ̣ⲉ̣[

19H

1   [   ] . . . [
2   [.]. ⲛⲉ ⲥϯⲉⲣⲱⲧⲉ̣ [ⲕⲉ]
3   ⲟ̣ⲩⲉⲓⲉ ⲥϯⲉⲃⲓⲱ ⲛ̄
4   ⲧⲱ[ⲧ̄ⲛ̄] ⲙ̄ⲧⲟⲛ ⲙ̄ⲙⲱ
5   ⲧⲛ̣ [ϩⲓⲧ]ⲛ̄ ⲧⲡⲩⲅⲏ ⲙ̄
6   [ⲡⲙⲟⲟⲩ] ⲙ̄ⲡⲱⲛ̄ϩ·
7   [   ]ⲧⲉⲉ̣ . .
8   [   ] . . . [

19F Left margin visible.   **2/3** Perhaps: п[ⲱ]ⲛ̄ϩ or п[ⲟⲩⲱ]ⲛ̄ϩ.   **8** ⲉⲉ perhaps: ⲥⲥ.
19H Left and right margins extant.   **3** There is ink between ⲉⁱ and ⲓ ; perhaps the left
half of a dieresis.   **4** ⲧ̄ⲛ̄, supralinear stroke is visible.   **5** ⲡⲩⲅⲏ apparent scribal error
for ⲡⲏⲅⲏ.

19F

1   [

2   the book of the [

3   [   ] They will not remember

4   his generation (γενεά),

5   since his [wife will]

6   be widowed (χήρα) [and his]

7   [children will be fatherless.]

8   [

19H

1   [

2   [   ] it (fem.) gives milk; [another]

3   one (fem.) gives honey.

4   [As for you (pl.)], rest

5   yourselves [by] the <spring>
     (π⟨η⟩γή) of

6   [the water] of life.

7–8   [

19F.3–6 Cf. Ps 109:9, 12–13, 15.   **19H.2–3** Cf. Exod 3:8; OdesSol 4:10.
5 "spring": lit. "rump."

20F

[ ]. .[.]ⲛ ⲇ̣ⲉ̣[
[ ]ⲡ̣ⲥⲱⲧⲏⲣ· ⲁϥϫ̣[
[ ]ⲉ ϩⲱⲥ ⲉϥⲟ ⲛ̄ϭⲁ̣[
[ ] ⲁ̣ϥⲡⲱⲧ’ ⲉϩⲟ̣ⲩ[ⲛ
[ ]ⲉ̣ ϫⲉ ⲡⲥⲱⲧ̣[ⲏⲣ
[ ]ⲱ̑ ⲓ̈ⲟⲩⲇ̣[ⲁⲥ
[ ]ⲟⲩϭⲁ[

20H

[. .].ⲉⲥ[.]. .[
ϫ̣ⲉ̣ ⲉⲣⲉⲥϩⲓⲙⲉ ⲛ̣[ⲓⲙ]
[ⲙ̄]ⲡⲓⲥⲧⲏ ⲛⲁⲥⲟ̣[
[. . .]ⲙ̣ⲉⲧⲁⲛⲟⲓ̈. [
[. . .]. ⲧⲟⲟⲧ̄ⲥ̄ [
[. . . .]ⲛ̄ⲥⲱⲟⲩ[
[. . . .]ⲙ̄ⲛ ⲉ . [

20F No margins visible. **6** ⲇ̣ perhaps: ⲗ. **20H.1** .[1] perhaps: ⲗ; .[2] perhaps: ⲉ. **3** ⲥⲟ̣[perhaps: ⲥⲱ[.

20F

1   [   ] and (δέ) [
2   [   ] the savior (σωτήρ). He [
3   [   ] as if (ὡς) he were [
4   [   ] He fled [
5   [   ] for the savior (σωτήρ) [
6   [   ] O (ὦ) [Jude
7   [

20H

1   [
2   [   ] since [every] faithful
     (πιστός)
3   woman will [
4   [   ] repent (μετανοεῖν) [
5   [   ] by her hand [
6   [   ] after them [
7   [

20F.6 Or: "[Judas."

21F

1   [   ] . ⲉⲕ[.]ⲁ̣[
2   [   ] . ⲉϩⲟⲩⲛ ϩⲁ ⲛ . [
3   [   ]̄.ϩ̄ ⲛ̄ⲅⲣ̄ϩⲁⲓ̈ⲃⲉⲥ[
4   [   ]ⲟ[.] . ⲉⲡⲁⲛⲧⲓⲕ . [
5   [   ]ⲉ[. .]ⲥ’ ⲉⲧⲉ ⲡⲁ[
6   [   ]ⲭⲉ ⲛ̄ⲏⲉ[
7   [   ]ⲕⲁⲧ̣[

21H

1   [   ] . [.]ⲅⲁⲣ[
2   [   ]ⲕⲟⲥⲙⲟⲥ, ⲟⲩ . [
3   [   ]ⲉ ⲡⲉ· ⲡⲉⲕⲱ̣ . [
4   [   ]ⲛ̄ⲧⲟϥ ⲛ̄ⲧ . [.]ⲁ[
5   [   ] . ⲁⲩ· ⲟⲩⲱ̣[.]ⲡ̣[
6   [   ] . ⲙ̇ⲏⲛ . [
7   [   ] . ϩ· [
8   [   ] . [

21F No margins visible.   **2** .¹ perhaps: ϥ, ⲣ.   **4** .² does not appear to be ⲣ.
21H No margins visible.   **3** ⲱ perhaps: ⲩ̣.   **6** .¹ not: ⲁ; .² perhaps: ⲥ.

21F

1   [

2   [   ] under [

3   [   ] and you (sg.) become (a)

shadow   [

4   [

5   [   ] which [

6–7   [

21H

1   [   ] for (γάρ) [

2   [   ] world (κόσμος) [

3   [   ] your (masc. sg.) [

4   [   ] he [

5–7   [

22F

1 [   ] . [
2 [ⲡ]ⲉⲩⲕⲏⲣⲩⲅⲙ[ⲁ
3 [ⲧ]ⲁϣⲉ ⲟⲉⲓϣ ϩ̣ ̄ [
4 [   ]ϩ̄ⲙ̄ ⲡⲕⲟⲥ[ⲙⲟⲥ
5 [   ]̄ . · ⲏ̄ ⲉⲧⲃ[ⲉ ⲟⲩ
6 [ⲉⲃⲟ]ⲗ ϩⲛ̄ ⲛ̄ⲥ . [
7 [   ] . ⲧⲉ[
8 [   ]ⲉⲕ[

22H

1 [.] . . ϩ̄ⲙ̄[ⲉⲓ]
2 ⲙⲏⲧⲓ ⲛ̄ⲧⲉⲧⲛ[
3 [.] . ⲧⲏⲩⲧⲛ̄ ⲙ̄[
4 [. . .]ϣⲱⲡⲉ· ⲡⲉ[
5 [. . .]ⲧⲡⲉ· ⲙ̄[ⲡⲣ̄]
6 [ⲧⲣ]ⲉⲟⲩⲁ̣’ ⲭ̣ⲟ[ⲟⲥ
7 [. . .] . ⲁϥ . [
8 [. . .]ⲉⲣⲟ̣[

22F No margins visible.   **22H** No margins visible.   7 . ¹ Perhaps: ⲩ, ⲭ.

22F

1	[
2	[their] proclamation
	(κήρυγμα) [
3	[ ] proclaim [
4	[ ] in the [world (κόσμος)
5	[ ] or (ἤ) why [
6	[from] the [
7–8	[

22H

1	[ ] in [
2	[ ] unless (εἰ μή τι) you (pl.) [
3	[ ] you (pl.)
4	[ ] happens [
5	[ ] the heaven. [Do not let]
6	anyone say [
7–8	[

23F

1   [   ] γn ακπ[
2   [   ]εn . . πεϥм . . [
3   [   ]oγ[ω]n̄ϩ εβoλ· . [
4   [   ] . [n]αcoγωnq̄[
5   [   ]τχωρα n̄n̄[
6   [   ]o n̄ε . ϯε[
7   [   ] . ω[

23H

1   [   ] . q ϩn̄ τϭ . [
2   [   ] . . ϣιπε· αγ[ω
3   [   ]ϩαï n̄nε . [.]αn[
4   [   ]n̄ ετn̄cτ . [.] . [
5   [   ]nhγ επεch[τ
6   [   ]πωρϣ̄ n̄n . [
7   [   ]κo[

23F No margins visible.   **6** Perhaps: n̄εcϯε[; cf. frg. 19H.2–3.   **23H** No margins visible.   **1** . ² perhaps: n, ι.   **7** o perhaps: ω, ϣ.

23F

1   [   ] you (sg.) [
2   [   ] his [
3   [   ] appear [
4   [will] know him [
5   [the] country (χώρα) of the [
6–7   [

23H

1   [   ] in the [
2   [   ] be ashamed. And [
3   [
4   [   ] your (pl.) [
5   [   ] coming below [
6   [   ] spread [
7   [

24F

1 [   ] . [
2 [   ]ⲉ ⲙ̄ⲡⲕⲟ[
3 [   ]ⲟⲩ ⲛⲁⲥ ⲉ[
4 [   ]ⲛⲧⲉⲥⲕ[
5 [ⲧ]ⲏⲣⲥ̄ ⲉⲧ[
6 [   ] · ⲁⲩⲱ ⲛⲥ̣[
7 [   ]ⲛⲱ[
8 [   ] . ⲁ2ⲏ[

24H

1 [   ] . ⲉ . ⲟⲛⲙ[
2 [   ]ϥⲧⲉⲣⲟ̣ . . [
3 [   ]ⲗⲓⲧⲣⲁ ⲛ̄[
4 [   ]ⲗⲓⲧⲣⲁ . [
5 [   ]ⲟⲉ ⲛ̄ⲗⲓⲧ[ⲣⲁ
6 [   ]ⲗⲓⲧ[ⲣⲁ
7 [   ]ⲱⲉ[
8 [   ] . . [

24F No margins visible.   **4** ⲉ perhaps: ⲑ.   **24H** No margins visible.   **5** ϥⲧ]ⲟ̣ⲉ, ⲧ]ⲟ̣ⲉ, or ⲥ]ⲟ̣ⲉ?

24F

1   [

2   [   ] of the [

3   [   ] to it (fem.) [

4   [

5   [   ] all [

6   [   ] and [

7–8 [

24H

1   [

2   [   ] he gives to [

3   [   ] pound (λίτρα) of [

4   [   ] pound (λίτρα) of [

5   [   ] pounds (λίτρα) [

6   [   ] pound (λίτρα) [

7–8 [

24H.3–6 John 12:3; 19:39.

25F

1   [   ]к[. . . .]оү[
2   [   ]ρω єιс 2н[нтє
3   [   ]аιϣοχнє є[
4   [   ]. моүоүт[
5   [   ]тєноү бє[
6   [   ]ϣωп[
7   [   ] . [.] . . . [

25H

1   [   ] ϥ[   ] . а[
2   [тєно]ү бє ⲱ̄ па[
3   [   ]ок 2ⲛ̄ оүє⁻ [
4   [   ]ⲉ̄ⲓ оп 2ⲛ̄ о[
5   [   ] . є2раї єп[
6   [   ]аүω[
7   [   ] . . [.] . [

26F

1   [   ]ωр̣ф̣[
2   [   ]λ а[. .]н[
3   [   ]к’ єво[λ
4   [   ]т̣ⲛ̄ . [

26H

1   [   ]пєϥ[
2   [   ]є[. .]ⲛ̣ρ̣[
3   [   ]ү· аⲛ[
4   [   ]є . . [

25F

1   [
2   [   ] behold [
3   [   ] I reflected concerning [
4   [   ] kill [
5   [   ] Now therefore [
6–7 [

25H

1   [
2   [Now] therefore O (ⲱ̂)
     my [
3   [   ] in a [
4   [   ] come again in [
5   [   ] up to the [
6   [   ] and [
7   [

26F

1–4 [

26H

1–4 [

27F

1   [   ]ṇ[
2   [   ]ṭ]ḥṝċ[
3   [   ]ϥṇ[
4   [   ]2 N̄[
5   [   ]M̄ⲱ[
6   [   ]ⲉⲱ[
7   [   ] . ⲉ· ⲡⲁ[
8   [   ]ⲉ . [

27H

1   [   ]ṇ[
2   [   ]ⲙⲁ[
3   [   ]ⲡⲟ . [
4   [   ]ⲉN̄ . [
5   [   ] . . . [
6   [   ]ⲛⲁ[
7   [   ]ẋⲉ N̄. [
8   [   ] . . [

27F

1   [
2   [   ] all [
3   [
4   [   ] in [
5–8   [

27H

1–8   [

28–30

illegible

Commentary

1:1–6: *Speech remnant one* (p. 97.13–30a)

The extant text begins on page 97, line 13, in the middle of a speech that continues to the middle of line 30. The identification of the first speaker is lost, but appears to be the central revelatory figure later identified as "the Savior" a title used in all eight occurrences in this gospel by the apostles when speaking about him in narration. Four or five independent sayings are found in 1:2–6. The first two sayings (1:2–3) may be clustered together because they are similar apocalyptic kingdom sayings. They were possibly preceded by an apostle's question concerning the kingdom, or another such kingdom saying by the Savior (cf. 1:1 "[the] kingdom"), suggesting a list of kingdom sayings in 1:1–3. These sayings evidence the influence of apocalyptic theology and traditions also found in Matthew's gospel, but it cannot be demonstrated at this point that the author simply copies Matthew's text.

The first saying (1:2) is extant only in its second half and concerns a now lost antecedent described as situated at the "right hand" of the apostles in the "kingdom of [the] heavens." A similar saying is found in Matt 20:21, where the mother of the sons of Zebedee asks Jesus that her sons, "may sit, one at your right hand and one at your left, in your kingdom," but the saying in 1:2 clearly indicates the lost antecedent is at the right hand of the apostles, who are portrayed as enthroned in apocalyptic positions of power.

The second saying (1:3) is a macarism (cf. frg. 9H.5b–7a) directed to any one "who will eat with me in the [kingdom] of the heavens." It is similar to the apocalyptic judgment sayings in Matt 8:11, Luke 13:29, and 22:30, where the images of eating and drinking in the kingdom, and the enthroned apostles judging the twelve tribes of Israel, are both set in a context of apocalyptic judgment. The saying is also attested in Luke 14:15 ("Blessed is the one who will eat bread in the kingdom of God"),[1] but the saying in 1:3 has two variants. The variant "with me," rather than "bread," provides a christological focus for the saying. The variant phrase "kingdom of the heavens" ultimately derives from Matthew's theological style and is employed throughout the Gospel of the Savior, rather than the more popular "kingdom of God."

The third saying (1:4) characterizes the apostles' influence as salt and light. This two stich saying is similar to the two sayings in Matt 5:13a, 14a, "You are

---

1. Luke 14:15, ⲚⲀⲓⲀⲧ︤ϥ̄ ⲘⲡⲈⲦⲚⲀⲞⲩⲰⲘ Ⲛ̄ⲞⲩⲞⲈⲓⲔ ⲌⲚ̄ ⲦⲘⲚ̄ⲦⲈⲢⲞ ⲘⲡⲚⲞⲩⲦⲈ. Quotations from the Coptic NT and its English translations are taken from *The Coptic Version of the New Testament in the Southern Dialect*, 7 vols., G. Horner, ed. (Oxford: Clarendon, 1911–1924). Quotations from the Greek NT are taken from *The Greek New Testament*, 3rd ed., corrected, Kurt Aland, Matthew Black, Carlo Martini, Bruce M. Metzger, and Allen Wikgren, eds. (Stuttgart: Deutsche Bibelgesellschaft, 1983).

the salt of the earth," and "You are the light of the world,"[2] where each stich in the Gospel of the Savior is followed by interpretive comments in Matt 5:13b, 14b–16, suggesting the form of the saying in the Gospel of the Savior may be more original. The second stich in the Gospel of the Savior also finds a parallel in the Gospel of Thomas (saying 24) with its concluding phrase attested in a variant form, "he lights up the whole world."[3]

The fourth saying (1:5) includes an ethical imperative, as the apostles, whose influence is to be as salt and light, are therefore neither to "sleep nor slumber." This phrase evokes a Gethsemane context for all of these sayings.[4] Although the name Gethsemane is not found on any of the fragments, that location is most probably the context for the sayings on the next page (cf. 4:2). This fragmentary fourth saying is either extended through line 30a, in which case there is no fifth saying, or concludes somewhere in the lacuna (lines 25–26a); in which case it is followed by a fifth saying (1:6) concerning "the garment of the kingdom." References to heavenly garments are found in a variety of apocalyptic texts and refer to the incarnated human spirit's ecstatic ascent to its original spiritual home in which a garment of fire or light replaces the fleshly body.[5] The perfect tense "I bought" refers to a past action, such as the Savior's previous heavenly descent, understood as the beginning of his death (see comments on 4:12), with his actual death on the cross still a future event.

The mixed metaphor concerning blood as "the blood of the grape" (lines 29–30) finds antecedents in early Jewish texts.[6] The saying in the Gospel of the Savior may be a reference to Gen 49:11b, where a connection is made in synonymous parallelism between blood of grapes, wine, and a garment, "he washes his garments in wine, and his robe in the blood of grapes." This saying appears to be a conflated version of the eucharistic sayings concerning the "blood of the covenant" and the "fruit of the vine," both in reference to the kingdom.[7] The saying provides the first extant allusion in this gospel to the passion, suggesting a mixture of visionary and eucharistic theologies (cf. 8:3).

1:7: *The apostle Andrew's question* (p. 97.30b–32)

The author uses a traditional editorial device to introduce the new speaker Andrew, but only the fragmented first word of Andrew's address is extant. His statement, or question, is lost in the lacuna.

---

2. Matt 5:13a, ⲚⲦⲰⲦⲚ Ⲡⲉ ⲠⲉϨⲘⲞⲨ ⲘⲠⲔⲀϨ; 5:14a, ⲚⲦⲰⲦⲚ Ⲡⲉ ⲠⲞⲨⲞⲉⲓⲚ ⲘⲠⲔⲞⲤⲘⲞⲤ.
3. GThom saying 24 (38,9): ϥⲢⲞⲨⲞⲉⲓⲚ ⲉⲠⲔⲞⲤⲘⲞⲤ ⲦⲎⲢϥ; cf. InterKnow 9,30–31a.
4. Cf. Mark 14:32–42.
5. Cf. 1 Enoch 62:15; 2 Enoch 22:5; 3 Enoch 12 and 15; ApocAb 13:14; TLevi 8:2; AscenIs 8:14–15, 26; 9:2, 17–18, 24–27; GPhil 57,18–22; 75, 20–24; 76, 25b–29a; ApocThom (Wilhelm Schneemelcher and Wilson) 2.750; AcThom 112:75–113:105 (="Hymn of the Pearl"); AcJohn 90; DSav 138:14b–139:8; 143:11–22; ApocPaul 22,24b–27a; GkApocPet 13 (Schneemelcher and Wilson, 2.633), 17–20 (2.635); 1 Cor 15:49.
6. Cf. Deut 32:14b; Sir 39:26b; 50:15a.
7. Cf. Mark 14:24–25; Matt 26:28–29; and Luke 22:18, 20.

2:12: *Speech remnant two* (p. 97.57–64)

When the text resumes, the Savior again is speaking. It is not clear whether the following third and fourth speech remnants (3:1–4; 4:1–12) are later portions of one speech initiated here and, thus, uninterrupted by apostles' questions. The subject has changed in speech remnant two from the apostles' behavior to the Savior's activity. It is not possible to determine whether his descent to Hades (2:1) includes a proclamation to the dead, but the reference to bound souls may indicate at least his purpose was to release those souls, a popular tradition found in numerous Jewish and Christian texts.[8]

The fragmentary second saying (2:2) introduces a transition with the resumptive phrase, "now therefore," a phrase that is spoken only by the Savior in extant portions of this text (4:1; 12:10; 13:5; frg. 25F.5; possibly also frg. 25H.2). The rest of the saying that begins in line 64 is lost.

3:1–4: *Speech remnant three* (p. 98.24–32)

The Savior is again speaking when the text resumes. It is not known whether this is a continuation of the preceding speech, possibly still in response to Andrew, or if there was an apostle's question or narrator's comment in the preceding lacuna to signal the beginning of a new speech. There appear to be four separate sayings in these nine lines; the first and last are fragmentary. Each of the first three sayings concludes with a Coptic adverbial construction, "with assurance" (3:1) and "with joy" (3:2–3), suggesting formal repetition as a literary device, as in poetry or hymnody (cf. the poetic section at frg. 5F.19b–32).

It is not clear in 3:1 whether the actor who does "everything" is the Savior, as in 3:2, or the apostles, as in 3:3. Saying 3:2 notes that the Savior will make a revelation to the apostles "with joy," but since its nature and concern is unstated, it is not clear whether that revelation occurs during the visions narrated later (cf. 7:1–7; 14:1–24) or whether it occurs in a section of text now lost. A small, unconnected fragment suggests the revelation possibly includes teaching (p. 122.60–63).

The fragmentary fourth saying (3:4) may be a Coptic translation of a Greek proverb, "For ($\gamma\acute{\alpha}\rho$) the person is unconditionally free ($\alpha\mathring{\upsilon}\tau\epsilon\xi o\acute{\upsilon}\sigma\iota o\varsigma$[9]) [who does such-and-such]." It is unclear whether the rest of the saying focused on a definition of freedom[10] or, instead, understood freedom specifically as the human spirit's independence from the material body, possibly through ascent.[11]

---

8. Cf. Psa 68:18; 107:14; Isa 49:9; 61:1; Odes Sol 17:12; 22:4; 42:14; ApocZeph 6:15; 10:4–5; 1 Pet 3:19; 4:6; GPet 10:41–42; EpApos 27; IgnMag 9:2; AscenIs 10:7–16; AcThom 10; GNic 21:3; ApocPaul 23,12–17; Iren, AdvHaer 5, 31:1–2.

9. Cf. $\alpha\mathring{\upsilon}\tau\epsilon\xi o\acute{\upsilon}\sigma\iota o\varsigma$ occurs once in LXX (Jer 34:16 [Sym.]).

10. Cf. GPhil 77,15–36.

11. Cf. 2 ApocJas 48,16–20; 59,1–11.

This latter sense may be indicated by the visionary ascents that the apostles will experience (7:1–7; 14:1–24) and by the next saying (4:1) which encourages them in the meantime, "[while] you (pl.) [are] in the body."

4:1–12: *Speech remnant four* (p. 98.10b–99.20a)

The text resumes with a transition ("now therefore"; 4:1; see comments on 2:2) introducing a series of about 12 sayings extending to 4:12.

Line 39 has the relatively uncommon sequence of the two letters oϫ between lacunae, yet this sequence is found nearby (3:4) in the word "unconditionally free" (ⲁⲩⲧⲟϫⲟⲩⲥⲓⲟⲥ). Also, the visually certain letters in lines 40–41 do not conform to any of the editor's usual formulas for introducing new speakers. These features suggest that the Savior's speech continued with the theme of freedom from 3:4 through 4:1.

The first extant saying (4:1) in this series begins with the resumptive phrase "now therefore," part of the Savior's style of instruction, indicating that he is again speaking and, apparently, drawing a conclusion. Here the apostles are warned to beware of the controlling effect of matter ($\H{u}\lambda\eta$) over the body ($\sigma\tilde{\omega}\mu\alpha$), possibly indicating an ascetic, or even a gnostic motif (see comments on 5F.19b–32), which might subtly permeate the entire text. Several of the Nag Hammadi texts, for example, demonstrate a similar ascetic tone, refer to the ruling effect of the passions over the body, and employ the terms $\H{u}\lambda\eta$ and $\sigma\tilde{\omega}\mu\alpha$ in close relation.[12]

The scribe's colon after the first saying and the first word of the second saying (4:2; the imperative "arise") indicate that a break occurs at the end of line 46. This suggests that this first saying (beginning with "now therefore") is a concluding exhortation to the preceding admonitions on freedom. Read in this way, the damaged text seems to indicate that the free person (3:4) is one who has control over bodily passions (4:1).

The second through fifth sayings (4:2–5) and the seventh saying (4:7) provide clear indications of plot, especially concerning time and place. In this gospel and in Matthew, Mark, and John, the second saying is spoken before the betrayal and arrest scenes. Saying 4:2 is nearly identical to Matt 26:46 and Mark 14:42,[13] but with the addition of a phrase attested in John 14:31, "Let us go away from this place."[14] The obscure mention of a "place" (ⲙⲁ) is likely a reference to Gethsemane.[15] The author appears to be conflating Matthew and

---

12. Cf. ApJohn 18,2–5; HypArch 96,15–22a; AuthTeach 31,8–32,16; Asclepius 66,9–11a; 66,35–67,11.

13. Note the simple imperative in Gospel of the Savior, ⲧⲱⲟⲩⲛ, rather than ⲧⲟⲩⲛ̄ ⲑⲏⲩⲧⲛ̄ in Matt 26:46, Mark 14:42, and John 14:31.

14. John 14:31 ⲙⲁⲣⲟⲛ ⲉⲃⲟⲗ ϩⲙ̄ ⲡⲉⲓⲙⲁ.

15. Cf. "a garden . . . a place ($\tau\acute{o}\pi os$; ⲙⲁ)" known by Judas (John 18:1–2); a "place" ($\chi\omega\rho\acute{\iota}ov$; but Coptic mss. read "garden" [ϭⲱⲙ]) called "Gethsemane" (Matt 26:36; Mark 14:32); and the "place" ($\tau\acute{o}\pi os$; ⲙⲁ) on the "Mount of Olives" (Luke 22:40).

John by inserting a Johannine element into a text and scene from Matthew. The mention of "the one who will hand me over,"[16] read in the light of Matt 26:46 (and Mark 14:42), suggests a possible reference to Judas, who might be mentioned in frg. 20F.66.

Sayings 4:3–5, 7 further situate this scene in the period before the Savior's arrest with their prophetic references to the fleeing apostles and the striking of the shepherd. The third saying (4:3) makes a reference to the fleeing of the apostles repeated in the fifth saying (4:5).[17] The fourth saying (4:4) states that the apostles will be "offended ($\sigma\kappa\alpha\nu\delta\alpha\lambda\acute{\iota}\zeta\epsilon\iota\nu$) by me," apparently a prediction to their future change of heart and flight of apostasy at the arrest of the Savior.[18] The presence of "by me" (ⲛ̅ϨⲎⲦ) in saying 4:4, and, "for it is written that" (ϥⲤⲎϨ ⲅⲁⲣ ⲭⲉ) in 4:7, indicate that 4:4 is derived from Matt 26:31, rather than Mark 14:27. Sayings 4:4 and 4:7 occur together as one saying, with a quote from Zechariah, in Matt 26:31; but in the Gospel of the Savior, they are separated by sayings 4:5 (cf. John 17:21) and 4:6 (cf. John 10:30), indicating again that the author is inserting Johannine elements into a text and scene from Matthew.

The fifth saying (4:5) continues the theme of the fleeing apostles, but also balances the Savior's abandonment with the assurance that God is nevertheless with him. Perhaps the saying is responding to a tradition that the crucified Savior was abandoned by God.[19] This is followed with the definite statement in the sixth saying, "I and my Father, we are a single one" (4:6), indicating the author's christological interest in the style of the Johannine tradition (cf. John 10:30; 17:21). Sayings suggesting an essential unity between the Father and the Savior are also found in Gnostic and related texts.[20]

In 4:7, the author returns to his theme of the fleeing apostles with a quotation formula introducing Zech 13:7. This indicates that the author's authorities are the Savior's sayings and at least one Old Testament prophetic quote, possibly more (cf. p. 121.28–33). The quotation is identical to Horner's Coptic text of Matt 26:31b, rather than the Coptic text of Zech 13:7,[21] again indicating that the author (or the translator from Greek to Coptic) is influenced by a Coptic version of Matthew. It is not clear whether the author wants the reader to understand the text of 4:7 as the author's commentary on the preceding sayings in the form of an aside, or as a saying of the Savior. If the author understands 4:7 as his own commentary, it is not clear whether he identifies with the

---

16. Cf. 1 ApocJas 25:7b–8a.

17. John's similar metaphor about the hireling shepherd who flees the wolf (John 10:5, 12–13; cf. 1 Enoch 89:26) is not part of the image in GSav 4:3 and 4:5, which instead follow the image of the fleeing sheep at the death of the shepherd (4:7; Zech 13:7).

18. Cf. AscenIs 3:14.

19. Cf. Matt 26:46; Mark 15:34; GPet 5:5.

20. Cf. TreatSeth 59,17–18; GPhil 74,22b–23; GThom 43,29–30.

21. See discussion and bibliography in Introduction.

authoritative narrative voice of Matthew, who in his own gospel repeatedly introduces the reader to Old Testament prophetic texts.[22] The same issue is raised in 13:18 where the author repeats an editorial aside from the Gospel of John. In both cases, it cannot be determined whether the author recognizes these are editorial comments, and not sayings, deriving from his source gospels. Thus, it remains unknown whether the author has a pseudepigraphic intent in identifying with the authoritative voices of Matthew and John. On the other hand, if the author understands 4:7 as a saying of the Savior, he transforms editorial comments from his source texts into sayings of the Savior.

The eighth saying (4:8a) is paralleled in John 10:11, but includes an extra word "yet" (ϭⲉ). The saying appears to have been inserted at this point due to the *Stichwort* "shepherd" in 4:7.

In the ninth saying (4:9), the author creates a two-stich saying in synonymous parallelism, by joining two phrases similar to John 15:13b, which uses the anonymous third person plural ("that he should lay down his life for his friends"). In contrast, GSav 4:9a personalizes the saying with the Savior speaking in the first-person singular and addressing the apostles in the second-person plural. The saying includes a future reference to the Savior's death on behalf of the apostles ("you [pl.]"), indicating the passage of time, and thus placing this scene in the period before the crucifixion. In 4:9b, the author moves beyond the shepherd imagery to direct the apostles to lay down their lives for their friends, as the Savior later will do, if they wish to be pleasing to "my father." The impersonal third-person singular and plural of John 15:13b is personalized in 4:9b to a second-person plural ("you [pl.]").

The tenth saying (4:10) is similar to sayings found in Mark 12:31, John 10:15b, and 15:12–13. The saying in John 15:13a refers to the "greater love," but, the saying in GSav 4:10 states that "no commandment is greater than this," perhaps under the influence of Mark 12:31b,[23] and John 15:13a.[24] 4:10 personalizes the actor as the Savior himself, who lays down his life "for people," rather than "one's friends" (John 15:13b), or the metaphorical "my sheep" (John 10:15b). It is unclear whether the saying reflects an encouragement to martyrdom.

The eleventh saying (4:11) describes the Savior's laying down of his life as the will of God,[25] which has already been "completed." The perfect tense may be a retrospective anachronism by the author, since the crucifixion has not yet occurred in this gospel. By reading the text this way, one understands the completion of the Father's will as the Savior's death on the cross. However, the

22. Cf. Matt 1:22–23; 2:5–6, 15–23; 4:14–16; 8:17; 12:17–21; 13:14–15, 35; 21:4–5; 26:54–56; 27:9–10.
23. Cf. Matt 22:36, 38.
24. Cf. "than this" (ⲉⲛⲁⲁ[ⲁ]ϥ ⲉⲧⲁⲓ) only in John 15:13a and GSav 4:10.
25. Cf. Matt 26:39b; Mark 14:36; Luke 22:42.

fragmentary twelfth saying (4:12)[26] suggests no anachronism, since the completion of the Father's will may well have begun earlier, perhaps with a previous descent from heaven,[27] so that for this author the heavenly descent was already the beginning of the Savior's death.[28]

Thus, the eighth through eleventh sayings possibly comprise a conceptual unit concerning self-sacrifice in behalf of others. If the three letter fragments (]ⲦⲈⲚ[) at the beginning of p. 99.24a are to be reconstructed as the transitional resumptive phrase ⲦⲈⲚ[ⲞⲨ ⳔⲈ] (see comments on 2:2, "now therefore"), then the Savior's speech on self-sacrifice may conclude somewhere in lines 24–26 before the transition is made to the apostles' next question, or the narrator's next comment, somewhere in lines 25–32.

5:1–2: *Apostles' questions* (p. 99.33–39a)

The apostles ask a question (5:1) concerning the time frame for something lost from the bottom of column 1, possibly a reference to his future return.[29] This is followed by another question (5:2) with a three-part sequence ("remember us, summon us, take us out") that may reflect the author's soteriology in a summary and programmatic form. Similar sequences, in whole or part, are used in other texts where a divine figure remembers his charges lost in a material world and then calls them out of it.[30] It is unclear whether these words refer to a parousia with a final eschatological ascent (cf. 1 Thess 4:16–17) or an imminent and occasional ecstatic ascent with the Savior; although the latter is suggested by the apostles' narrations of their two ecstatic ascents (7:1–7; 14:1–24).

6:1–2: *Speech remnant five* (p. 100.1–6a)

After what may be the last word ("[by] sight") of a question by the apostles, or a comment by the narrator, an editorial quotation formula (lines 1b–2a) signals a shift to another speech by the Savior, but only the opening address is extant. The address provides the first of three uses in this gospel of the exclamatory address, "O, my holy members ($\mu\epsilon\lambda o\varsigma$)," the Savior's characteristic phrase that refers in the Gospel of the Savior to the apostles as a group (cf. p. 107.50–51; frg. 9H.4–5). The phrase is also found in the Greek Apocalypse of Paul and may ultimately derive from its mystical use in Pauline ecclesiology.[31] Only here is the phrase followed by the complementary address "my seeds"

---

26. Cf. TeachSilv 110,18b–19a.
27. Cf. John 1:14a; Phil 2:5–11.
28. Cf. GPhil 53,6b–9.
29. For other options to similar questions, cf. John 16:16–19 (return as spirit); EpApos 16 (return as judge); HypArch 96,32 (revelation of the spirit of truth).
30. Cf. DSav 135,20b–136,1a; 140,7b–9; 2 ApocJas 46,9–19; ApocAdam 69,19–24; 72,1–9; ApJas 9,1b–4; for a five-part sequence, cf. GThom 32,14b–19a.
31. GkApocPaul 51 (Schneemelcher and Wilson, 2.742); cf. 1 Cor 6:15; 12:12–31; Rom 12:3–5; Eph 4:25; 5:30; IgnEph 4:2; Trall 11:2.

($\sigma\pi\acute{\epsilon}\rho\mu\alpha$), an unusual designation for the apostles.[32] The Savior's speech is con-cluded in the lacuna, as is indicated by the change to a speech by a spokesman for the apostles when the text resumes at 7:1.

7:1–7: *Apostles' vision remnant one* (p. 100.33–53)

The text resumes in mid-sentence in 7:1, as the apostles narrate a visionary ascent they experienced "upon the mountain,"[33] apparently the Mount of Olives (see comments on "this place" at 4:2).[34] This is the first clear indication of apocalyptic visionary ascent in this gospel. Here the apostles "too became like the spiritual bodies," that is, they were transformed with the Savior,[35] in con-trast to the transformation story in the synoptic gospels, where Jesus alone is transformed on the mountain before the bystanders Peter, James, and John.[36] The apostle Paul speculated on heavenly and earthly bodies[37] and even men-tioned his own, or an acquaintance's ecstatic ascent to "the third heaven," but would not divulge details.[38]

The apostles' sight was unlimited in their spiritual bodies (7:2), a theme shared with other transformation and ascent texts.[39] They then ascend in a man-ner similar to Enoch[40] and describe an apparent conflict in which the heavens "[rose] up against each other" (7:3), suggesting a heavenly disturbance, perhaps due to their ascent.[41] The transformed and ascended apostles observe the fear-ful reactions of two types of heavenly beings, the watchers[42] and the angels. The watchers were apparently disturbed by the ascent of the apostles past the heav-enly gates which they guard, and the rising up of the heavens against each other (7:3–4).[43] The angels were also afraid and fled (7:5). The apostles are eyewit-nesses, after the event, that the Savior "pierced [through] all the heavens" (7:6) and thus, in his function as Savior, he opened the gates of the heavens for the ascent of his followers.[44] This scene might provide an interpretive context for the apostles' earlier request to the Savior to "remember us, summon us, and take us out of the world" (5:2), since the Savior's piercing of all the heavens can be understood as the activity by which he can take them "out of the world."

32. Cf. "he is the shepherd of the seed," in On Anoint. 40,18–19a.
33. Cf. Exod 24:9–18; TLevi 2:5–7; Mark 9:2–4; GkApocPet 15 (Eth = 4.) (Schneemelcher and Wilson, 2.633).
34. Cf. Matt 26:30, 36.
35. Cf. DSav 132,5b–12a; GPhil 58,3b–10a; 61,20b–35; 78,25–79,13; Zost 4,20–7,22.
36. Cf. Matt 17:1–8; Mark 9:2–4; Luke 9:28–36; 2 Pet 1:18.
37. Cf. 1 Cor 15:35–50.
38. Cf. 2 Cor 12:1–4; Matt 17:9; Mark 9:9–10a.
39. Cf. the Strasbourg Papyrus, Copt. 6, verso, p. 158 (Schneemelcher and Wilson, 1.105); GPhil 61,20b–35.
40. Cf. 1 Enoch 14:8–9.
41. Cf. ApJas 15,5b–13a; Rev 12:7; ApocAb 18:8–10; AscenIs 7:9; 10:29.
42. Cf. Dan 4:10–20; 1 Enoch 1–36.
43. Cf. 1 Enoch 1:4; Zost 4,20–31.
44. Cf. Eph 6:12–13; Col 2:15.

Four lost pages (pp. 101–104 = 8 columns = 256 lines)

The codicological analysis (see Introduction) demonstrates that one codex sheet with 256 lines is missing at this point, and for which the scribe's pagination was 101–104. When the text resumes with 8:1–4 (= p. 105), only lines 5–16a have legible text, though very fragmentary. Where the legible text does resume in line 5 there is a change of voice and topic from the apostles' narration of their vision, to the Savior and his sayings.

8:1–4: *Speech remnant six* (p. 105.5–16)

The Savior is again addressing the apostles in 8:1–4. Although the text is heavily damaged, the general sense of the passage seems clear. There are at least four fragmentary sayings in these twelve lines, the fourth saying (8:4) is too fragmentary for any detailed analysis, and only the third (8:3) is complete. The first three sayings appear to share a similar structural form, making comparisons between individuals who will or will not act acceptably in relation to an unidentified concern. The focus is possibly the eucharist, as is made explicit in the third saying.

The restored "Amen," followed by a period (line 7a), signals the end of the first saying (8:1). The second and third sayings (8:2–3) also conclude with "Amen."[45] The first two sayings (8:1–2) are similar to the saying in Rev 3:20,[46] and in the Gospel of the Savior they also appear to be apocalyptic sayings, but are set into a eucharistic context (8:3), suggesting an apocalyptic interpretation of traditional eucharistic symbols and language (cf. 1:6).

When compared against Nestle's Greek text of Rev 3:20, Horner's Sahidic Coptic text evidences a widespread shift from the Greek's personal second-person singular ("you [sg.]") to the Coptic's impersonal third-person singular ("him"). This shift in person between the Greek and Coptic traditions of Rev 3:20 seems to be reflected here in GSav 8:1–2. This suggests the possibility that 8:1–2 may contain two sayings which are structurally similar to the Coptic form of the saying in Rev 3:20, but there is not enough text to argue that 8:1–2 may contain an independent attestation (variant form) of Rev 3:20.

For example, the first stich of Rev 3:20 in Coptic ("if anyone should hear my voice") is structurally similar to the damaged first stich of GSav 8:1 ("] that one who will [") and 8:2 ("] that one who [. . .] to me [").[47] The second stich of Rev 3:20 ("I will go in to him, eat with him, and he with me") is structurally the same as the damaged second stich of both GSav 8:1 ("] I will [. . . .] with him myself["), and 8:2 ("] I will cause him [. . .] with me").[48] The verbs have been lost to lacunae.

45. Note the recurring "Amen" in the hymn in AcJohn 94–96, where the apostles respond "Amen" to the Savior's verses.
46. "If anyone should hear my voice and open the door, I shall go in unto him and eat with him, and he with me" (Rev 3:20).
47. Note the extra phrase in Rev 3:20a, "and open the door."
48. Note the extra phrases in Rev 3:20b, "eat with him, and he with me."

The apparently positive images of apocalyptic fellowship with the Savior in 8:1–2, introduce in 8:3 a two-stich saying with a negative image concerning a refusal to accept the eucharist. Two similar sayings are found in John 6:54, 56. The first stich in 8:3 is antithetic to two identical sayings in John 6:54a and 6:56a ("those who eat my flesh and drink my blood"), but is formulated in a manner similar to John 12:48 ("*That one who* rejects me and *does not receive my* word"). Whereas the second stich in John 6:54b refers to a reward ("will have eternal life"), the second stich of 6:56b refers to a relationship ("[will] abide in me and I in them"), as does the second stich in GSav 8:3 ("this one is a stranger to me"). Thus, 8:3 is an antithetically formulated attestation of the content of John 6:56.[49]

This third saying (8:3) contains the second allusion to the eucharist in this gospel (cf. 1:6), but how the eucharist is understood, whether gnostic or orthodox, is unclear.[50] Saying 8:3 possibly demonstrates the author's first contact with a tradition elsewhere attested in Rev 14:8–9. It is possible that this speech (8:1–4) originally continued with the text of 5H.23–24.[51]

9:1–2: *Speech remnant seven* (p. 105.40–49)

The first extant saying (9:1) employs the second-person singular, which is used by the Savior when addressing the cross. The mention of "the cross" (9:1–2) and the use of "Amen" (9:1), two words that are always used by the Savior in the extant fragments of the Gospel of the Savior (where the speaker can be identified), support the suggestion that the Savior is speaking to the cross in 9:1, and possibly in 9:2 as well.

The phrase "those on (the) [right] [apart from] those on (the) [left]" (9:2) is similar to passages found in early Jewish apocalyptic texts in which humanity is shown to be judged and separated into two groups, the evil on the left and the righteous on the right. The separation is here effected by the shadow of the cross, but it also can be effected by the Garden (variant "Tree") of Eden,[52] or by a spring of water with light upon it,[53] or by the moon's path which separates light from darkness, the righteous from sinners.[54]Other early Christian texts also identify the actual cross, or a metaphysical cross, as the cause of the separation,[55] demonstrating an exegetical development of the canonical crucifixion passages[56] in relation to the images of judgmental separation inherited from the

---

49. Such is the case, regardless of their differences in number, singular in GSav 8:3, and plural in John 6:56.

50. On gnostic conceptualizations of the eucharist, see GPhil 56:26b–57:22a; 75:14b–24; cf. Jude 12; Iren, AdvHaer 5.2.1–3; On orthodox conceptualizations, see Did 9–10, 14; 1 Clem 40–41; IgnEph 13; IgnPhd 4; IgnSm 7–8; Justin, 1 Apol 65–67; DialTrypho 41.

51. See the Introduction ("Codicological Analysis") for a discussion of the position of fragment 5 among the fragments.

52. Cf. ApocAbr 21:7; 22:3–5; 27:1–2; 29:4–6, 11–12.

53. Cf. 1 Enoch 22:8–13.

54. Cf. the cosmic hymn alluding to Gen 1:4b in 1 Enoch 41:8–9.

55. Cf. AcJohn 98–100; GPhil 67,24–25; cf. 53,13b–23a; 60,26–28a.

56. Cf. Mark 15:27; Matt 27:38; Luke 23:32–43; John 19:18.

Jewish apocalyptic tradition.[57] It is possible that this portion of the Savior's speech originally continued with the text of 5H.51–64.[58]

10:1–3: *Speech remnant eight* (p. 106.9–16)

The first extant saying (10:1) probably continues to the scribe's punctuation mark in the middle of line 13. This saying is addressed to an individual[59] whose identity is lost in the lacuna in line 10a. It is unclear whether the speaker is the Savior addressing an apostle whose name could fit into the lacuna (e.g., Jude or Judas as in frg. 20F.6), or addressing the cross (cf. 5H.53–64; 5F.19–32), since the scribe's abbreviation for "cross" can fit into the space of the lacuna in line 10a; but the speaker could also be an apostle, or even the cross,[60] addressing an unidentified individual. It is not possible that it is addressed to the apostles as a group because the person addressed is singular and the apostles' usual designation in this text ("O, my holy members," see comment on 6:2) is too large for the available space in line 10a.

The first saying begins with an injunction not to weep, but rather to "rejoice and understand." Such exhortative language suggests the Savior is speaking (cf. 13:13). It is not clear whether "Lord" (ϫⲟⲉⲓⲥ) is to be understood in reference to the Father (cf. 12:6) or the Savior (cf. 1:7; 12:3, 4). The divine title "Lord" is possibly the antecedent for the third-person singular pronominal prefixes ("he," ϥ-) in lines 12b and 14b, and which apparently refer to a positive action that either the Father or the Savior will perform so that the individual addressed need not weep.

The second saying (10:2) probably begins after the scribe's punctuation mark (line 13) and ends with the word "Amen" (line 15), apparently referring to what the Father, or the Savior, will do so that the unidentified individual can rejoice.

The following Coptic ordinal "the second" (10:3) indicates that an enumeration was initiated earlier in a now lost portion of text. The speaker cannot be identified. It is possible that this portion of text is an editorial comment rather than a saying, and originally continued into the poetic sayings in 5F.19–32, if frg. 5F is construed as the bottom part of p. 106.[61]

11:1–2: *Speech remnant nine* (p. 106.39–47)

The Savior is again speaking when the text resumes in 11:1. The first saying (11:1) has lost the antecedent to the third-person plural prefix, which refers to an unidentified group (possibly Israel, or people in general). This group looks to "you (sg.)," probably a reference to the cross (cf. 11:2), and they are divided

57. Cf. Matt 25:32–34, 41.
58. See the Introduction ("Codicological Analysis") for a discussion of the position of fragment 5 among the fragments.
59. Note the conjunctive singular ⲛ̄ⲣ- in line 11b.
60. Cf. the speaking cross in GPet 10:42.
61. See the Introduction ("Codicological Analysis") for a discussion of the position of fragment 5 among the fragments.

by their reactions.[62] It appears that the cross is again described as having a judgmental function over people (cf. 9:1–2).

The second saying (11:2) is clearly addressed to the cross, just as the apostle Andrew addresses the cross before his own crucifixion in the Acts of Andrew,[63] or as the voice from heaven addresses the cross at the resurrection in the Gospel of Peter.[64] The attitude of being "eager" (literally, "to be earlier than," and, thus, "to anticipate in reference to an event"[65]) suggests perhaps a willingness to grasp one's destiny, not only on the part of the Savior (cf. 5H.61b–63), but also on the part of the cross. The Savior's speech to the cross ends somewhere in the column's lost lower half, as is indicated by his address to the apostles when the text resumes at the top of the next column (cf. plural "you," in 12:2).

12:1–2: *Speech remnant ten* (p. 107.1–4a)

The longest and most continuous portion of text is on fragment 1 with four consecutive and nearly intact columns across both sides of one leaf, pages 107 and 108.

The first saying (12:1) is extant only in its conclusion with "see them," possibly a reference to heavenly phenomena seen in a vision, as the following texts suggest. The second saying (12:2) draws a conclusion (cf. "therefore," line 2) from the Savior's lost preceding words indicating a theme common to visionary ascent texts, that a fuller revelation of the Savior may cause the viewers to be "disturbed" because of the revelation's supernatural character, a danger to mortal beings still in fleshly bodies (see comments on 12:4). The four occurrences of the verb "to see" in 12:1–5, indicate that his revelation is something they will visually experience.

12:3–4: *Apostles' questions/comments* (p. 107.4b–23a)

A standard quotation formula "we said to him" (line 4), and the mention of John (line 10), identifies the group of speakers as two or more of the apostles. This plural voice asks two questions related to the Savior's preceding comment about his self-revelation. The first concerns the "form" in which he will reveal himself to them; the second concerns the "kind of body" in which he will come (12:3).[66] The two questions are synonymous rather than antithetic, since a potential distinction between the two (form vs. kind of body) is not noted. "Form" and "kind" synonymously refer to the distinction between an earthly body of flesh and a heavenly body of spirit, existing as two different forms or kinds, and so the apostles' question concerns the nature of his spiritual body. This is similar to early

---

62. Cf. Matt 27:29–31; Mark 15:18–20; Luke 23:27.
63. Acts of Andrew (Schneemelcher and Wilson, 2.148).
64. GPet 10:42.
65. Cf. ApJas 7,12–14,35b–38; Acts of Andrew (Schneemelcher and Wilson, 2.148).
66. Cf. 1 Cor 15:35–44; EpApos 16 (Schneemelcher and Wilson, 1.258).

Jewish traditions where the Glory (Kavod) of God is visible to humans, especially visionaries, as fire and bright light,[67] and can also be revealed in a human-like image.[68] Another metaphor besides transformation is that of the "putting on" of the new body as a garment (cf. 1:6, "the garment of the kingdom").

It is unclear whether the double occurrence of the word "come" (12:3–4) indicates a parousia in the sense of an eschatological descent from heaven,[69] or, instead, indicates his ecstatic and revelatory transformation during the apostles' ecstatic ascent with him (cf. 14:1–16).[70] The question is odd, considering their previous ecstatic transformation, ascent, and visual observation of the ascended Savior (7:1–7), an experience that presumably would answer such questions.

The issue of his form or kind of body is again raised in John's concern that the glory of the Savior's self-revelation[71] might correspond to the apostles' mortal ability to experience and understand it (12:4).[72] Their "despair from fear" is John's primary concern.[73] Some early Jewish apocalyptic traditions understood that if mortal bodies viewed the Glory of God without prior transformation, as, for example, Enoch experienced,[74] they could be harmed or even destroyed.[75]

12:5–10: *Speech remnant eleven* (p. 107.24–53)

The author employs a standard editorial formula (12:5a) to begin another speech by the Savior. What follows is a series of approximately six sayings. The first saying (12:5b) continues the theme of fear and concludes with the comment "in order that you might see and believe." Seeing and believing are closely related in the Gospel of the Savior and their order is logical: a vision of his self-revelation, however threatening to their mortal nature, will lead to belief. Although the object of belief is unstated, it seems that they are to believe that he is the descended Savior who will guarantee their safe transformation, ecstatic ascent, and final eschatological ascent to the Father (cf. 5:2). Their visual observation of his ecstatic ascent may be the basis for that belief, as suggested by the two similar authoritative eyewitness statements made during their visions (7:6 and 14:5).

---

67. Cf. Exod 16:10b; 24:17; 40:38; Lev 9:23–24; 1 Kings 8:10–11.

68. Cf. Gen 1:26; Exod 33:18–34:8 (LXX); Ezek 1:26–28; 8:2; 1 Enoch 14:20–22; 2 Enoch 22:1; Mark 9:2b–3.

69. Cf. 1 Thess 4:15–16.

70. Cf. GThom saying 37.

71. Cf. John 1:14; 17:24; Strasbourg Papyrus, Copt. 6, recto, p. 157.

72. Cf. 2 ApocJas 54,19–20; GPhil 57,28b–58,10a; Phil 3:21.

73. Cf. 1 Enoch 60:1–4; ApocAb 11:1–6; SophJesChr 91,10–24a; GMary 10,9–15a; Mark 9:6; Matt 17:6–7; Luke 9:34.

74. Cf. 3 Enoch 15:1–2.

75. E.g., blinded (cf. Philo, *De Fuga et Inventione* 165, in F.H. Colson and G.H. Whitaker, trans. [Loeb Classical Library; London: William Heinemann Ltd.; Cambridge: Harvard University Press, 1934], 5.99–100) or, burned up (cf. *Heikhalot Rabbati* 3.4, in S.A. Wertheimer, *Batei Midrashot* [Jerusalem, Mossad Harav Kook, 1968], vol. 1).

The second saying (12:6) is a version of a saying attested in John 20:17. It begins with the adversative conjunction "but indeed" (ἀλλά) and a prohibition against touching the Savior, a theme alluded to in gnostic texts,[76] suggesting that the previous saying excludes belief on the basis of physical contact with the Savior, in favor of belief based on visionary experience. This appears to be contrary to the position of the Gospel of John, where the disciples cannot participate in an ecstatic ascent with him[77] and where belief is based on physical contact or, at least, on participation in an apostolic tradition initiated by the Savior's physical contact with eyewitnesses.[78] The rest of the second saying refers to his ascent. The prohibition against touching him is in effect "until" his ecstatic visionary ascent to the Father, God, and Lord. In John 20:17, it is spoken to Mary Magdalene (see comments on frg. 20H.2–6) during a post-mortem resurrection appearance and in reference to his resurrected body, which is not to be touched. In John 20, he tells Mary to tell "my brothers" that he is ascending "to my Father and your Father, to my God and your God." However, in the Gospel of the Savior, he himself speaks the saying directly to the apostles and before his second ecstatic ascent (14:5),[79] and with the additional phrase "and my Lord who is your Lord."

The third saying (12:7) appears to be both an invitation that they too can be transformed, that is, that they will "burn" with glorified bodies if they are near him through ascent (cf. 7:1; 14:3), and a warning that mortal beings will burn unless they are first transformed (see comments on 12:4).

The fourth saying (12:8) is an ego-proclamation that provides the reason for the third saying; one "will burn" because the Savior himself is "the fire that blazes." Similar descriptions of divine beings as fire were employed in reference to God[80] and to transformed bodies of glory, such as that of Enoch,[81] indicating that the Savior's ego-proclamation can be understood as a self confession of deity.

The fifth saying (12:9) further extends the fire imagery and connects it to the third saying's theme of nearness (12:7; cf. frg. 11.31–32). The synonymous parallelism of the saying's two stiches suggests that "fire" and "life" are equivalent. This saying is found with a variant in the Gospel of Thomas, saying 82, "Jesus said, 'He who is near me is near the fire, and he who is far from me is far from the kingdom'" (GThom 47,17–19; see the Introduction).

The incomplete sixth saying (12:10) appears to be the last saying in this series. This is indicated by the transitional resumptive phrase "now then" and the narrator's comment which follows (13:1). The admonition that they gather to

76. Cf. ApJas 7,35b–38; 1 ApocJas 32,6–12; 2 ApocJas 56,14–15; 57,10–19; TTruth 74, 21–30.
77. Cf. John 7:33–34; 8:21; 13:33, 36.
78. Cf. John 20:24–29; 1 John 1; Matt 28:9.
79. Cf. ApJas 9,15.
80. Cf. Ezek 1:26–27.
81. Cf. 3 Enoch 15:1.

him continues the logic of the preceding five sayings, that nearness to him involves the promise of a vision of God's glory.

13:1: *Narrator's comment* (p. 107.54–57a)

This section contains the fragmentary remains of an editorial transition formula in the voice of the narrating apostles (cf. "to us," line 58a), introducing the Savior as speaker. It does not appear that an apostle's question was asked in lines 53–57a.

13:2–18: *Speech remnant twelve* (p. 107.57b–108.64)

This speech appears to be comprised of sixteen sayings followed by the narrator's comment (13:18). The first saying (13:2) is introduced by one of the author's editorial formulas "[He said] to us," and refers to the Savior "[as] a child" in their midst, possibly in the sense of Matt 18:1–5 and 19:13–15. However, in InThom 8.1b, the divine child Jesus once speaks as does the Savior in the Gospel of the Savior, that is, as a sent heavenly redeemer (GSav 13:11) who descended to call people to heavenly things (5:2). In the Coptic Apocalypse of Paul (18,3–22), Paul's guiding spirit and interpreting angel also is a child (called "the holy spirit") who ascends with the apostle on a tour of heaven, as do the apostles and the Savior in the Gospel of the Savior (p. 122.60–63). In the Acts of John (88), James and John see Jesus in the form of a child who calls them.

The second saying (13:3) is introduced by another of the author's editorial formulas "he said" (line 57) and the speaker is probably the Savior (cf. 13:1). The saying begins with an introductory "Amen," apparently as a proleptically affirmative oath in the sense of "truly."[82] The introductory "Amen" in the canonical gospels is spoken 74 times and only by Jesus,[83] and is accompanied by a phrase like, "I say to you." A single "Amen," without the accompanying phrase, is also attested as a proleptically affirmative oath in much older Hebrew texts.[84] The saying concerns the short time that he will be with them. This sense of urgency is elsewhere mentioned in the Gospel of the Savior in relation to a possible gnostic conception of the imminent restoration of the Pleroma (see comments on 5F.19b–32). Thus, this second saying possibly suggests that they must experience pre-mortem ecstatic ascent with him soon if they wish to find their way to their spiritual home after death.[85] This saying may be a visionary reinterpretation of similar sayings in John 7:33, 13:33a and 14:19, where he will soon go to the Father, but, contrary to the Gospel of the Savior, they will not be able to follow through ecstatic ascent.

82. Cf. Matt 18:3, also in a context concerning children.
83. E.g., Matt 5:18.
84. Cf. 1 Kgs 1:36 (Heb., אמן; LXX [3 Kgs 1:36] γένοιτο); Jer 28:6 (Heb., אמן; LXX [Jer 35:6] ἀληθῶς).
85. Cf. GPhil 56,15b–19.

The third saying (13:4) is introduced by another quotation formula, "[he] replied" (lines 63b–64). The author of the Gospel of the Savior consistently uses the word "reply" (ⲟⲩⲱϣⲃ) to introduce a response to a comment or a question from a previous speaker, thus raising the possibility that an apostle's question was asked in the preceding lacuna (lines 53–56); however, here it may be employed as a phrase synonymous with "he said" (ⲡⲉϫⲁϥ), already used twice in the preceding seven lines (lines 57 and 61), so that its use here may be dictated by the author's concern for stylistic variety. This third saying continues on the next page[86] where the discussion has changed to the subject of the opposition to the Savior. This suggests that the author knew narrative traditions of the plot against Jesus and those who "took counsel against him."[87] The beginning and central sections of the saying are lost, but the scribe's period in the middle of line 5 indicates the saying's conclusion, where the Savior states that he is a stranger "to him" (or, "to it"). This phrase suggests an essential enmity between two individuals.[88] The antecedent to the pronoun is lost in the lacuna and so can be identified with either "the plan" (line 1), or, more likely, a person such as Judas (cf. 4:2b; 20F.6), referred to as a "stranger" to the Savior.

The fourth saying (13:5) continues the passion theme in reference to the Savior's suffering. The saying parallels the theological statement in 1 Pet 3:18, which looks retrospectively at the suffering of the Savior. This fourth saying has the same content, but as a saying of the Savior expressing his present, or imminent experience. The text of this gospel is too fragmentary to indicate the author's understanding of "the [sins] of the world," but the general dualistic orientation of the text might suggest sins are understood to be any involvement with material existence (cf. 4:1; 13:14). The scribe's period at the end of line 8 concludes the saying.

In the fifth saying (13:6), the Savior rejoices over the behavior of the apostles, in contrast to his grieving over the sins of the world in the previous saying. The sixth saying (13:7) draws a conclusion from the logic of the preceding sayings with a resumptive "therefore" emphasizing the ideal attitude and activity of the apostles who are encouraged that he will rejoice over their work.

The seventh saying (13:8) is comprised of a series of three ego-proclamations concerning kingship,[89] with at least the first two concluded by "Amen." The scribe's period in the middle of line 23 indicates the conclusion to the tripartite seventh saying. The eighth saying (13:9), which probably begins after the period in line 23, is mostly lost and concluded with "Amen" in line 26a, as indicated by another period.

The ninth (13:10) and tenth sayings (13:11) share a common structure; each is a two stich saying completed by "Amen"; the first stich refers to the Savior's

---

86. Cf. p. 108.1.
87. Cf. Matt 12:14; Mark 3:6.
88. Cf. GkApocPaul 16 (Schneemelcher and Wilson, 2.722).
89. Cf. Mal 1:14.

action and the second stich to the apostles' action on the same issue, whether contending (13:10) or being sent (13:11). Further, the ninth saying reflects an unidentified conflict in which the Savior fights for the apostles, possibly understood as the visionary's spiritual fight against the evil heavenly powers engaged during ascent (cf. 7:4).[90] In the tenth saying, the Savior notes that he has been sent, presumably by the Father, and that he now wishes to send the apostles.[91] Although the reason for sending them is not known, a few passages in the Gospel of the Savior seem to indicate that their mission is to teach the way of ecstatic pre-mortem ascent,[92] just as he teaches them (12:5–10; p. 122.60–63), thus providing a mythic rationale for the writing of the Gospel of the Savior: the transmission of visionary apostolic teaching.

In the eleventh saying (13:12), the Savior announces to the apostles "joy for the world."[93] The masculine antecedent of the pronoun "it" (line 42) is unclear; it may be the "joy" which they may anticipate entering,[94] or "the world," which is in closer proximity to the pronoun and which is developed next in 13:14–15. Thus, although they are physically in the world (13:6b), they are not to let it overcome them (13:14b; cf. 4:1), and should be free from it (13:15).

The twelfth saying (13:13) repeats the idea that the apostles are not to weep, but are to rejoice (cf. 10:1), and the reason is given in the next two sayings. Like the ninth and tenth sayings, the thirteenth (13:14) and fourteenth (13:15) sayings share a common structure and parallel themes. Each is a two stich saying followed by "Amen," with the first stich referring to the Savior's action and the second encouraging the apostles to specific actions: overcoming the world (13:14) and being free from it (13:15).[95]

The first stich of the fourteenth saying is also found in John 16:33c and the unidentified gospel of the Strasbourg Papyrus.[96] But the version of the saying in the Gospel of the Savior has a second stich in lines 47–49, that forms with the first stich a chiasm in synonymous parallelism. This saying on overcoming the world is preceded by an admonition that they rejoice in GSav 13:13b and the Strasbourg Papyrus, but not in John.

The issues raised in the fifteenth and sixteenth sayings (13:16–17), and in the narrative comment (13:18), are not directly related to the preceding sayings, and seem to parallel the same chronological order as the passion events described in John 19:28–35. The fifteenth saying (13:16) possibly refers to the drinking by the Savior on the cross;[97] if so, it is predictive since the crucifixion

90. Cf. John 18:36; Eph 6:10–17; GThom 41,31–42,7a; 1 ApocJas 32,23a–34,20a; GMary 15,1–17,7a.
91. Cf. John 17:18; 20:21b.
92. Cf. GPhil 66,16b–21a.
93. Cf. Luke 2:10.
94. Cf. Matt 25:21–23; GPhil 65,27–30.
95. Cf. John 8:36.
96. Cf. Coptic 5, verso.
97. Cf. John 19:28–29; Matt 27:34; Mark 15:23; GPet 5:16.

is still future. But, the saying's mention of drink, life (ⲱⲛⲍ̄), and rest (Ⲙ̄ⲧⲟⲛ), finds perhaps a closer conceptual parallel at frg. 19H.4b–6, "rest (Ⲙ̄ⲧⲟⲛ) yourselves [by] the spring (π⟨η⟩γή) of the water of life (ⲱⲛⲍ̄)." This suggests that drinking may be a metaphor for spiritual transformation, so that the image of Jesus drinking on the cross is given a visionary reinterpretation in the Gospel of the Savior as a spiritual transformation associated with ascent.[98] The sixteenth saying (13:17) predicts the piercing[99] of the crucified Savior with a lance,[100] a future reference clearly indicating the crucifixion has not yet occurred.

This list of sixteen sayings is then followed by a comment from the narrator (13:18), who possibly speaks in the guise of the author of the Gospel of John.[101] This possibility is supported by the centrality of John in the dialogue with the Savior concerning the Savior's glory (12:2–10), and especially by the numerous parallels to Johannine texts, language, and concepts. However, the same has been said in this commentary about the author's possible use of Matthew's narrating voice and the Gospel of the Savior's numerous parallels to the Gospel of Matthew (see comments at 4:7). Thus, if the authoritative narrating voices from the Gospel of Matthew and the Gospel of John are appropriated by the author of the Gospel of the Savior, then this might indicate that the authoritative names supporting this gospel were both Matthew and John, or, more likely, would have been all the apostles. Thus, in reference to a functional title, and in relation to genre and authority (name), this text might originally have been promoted as the Gospel of the Apostles, or the Apocalypse of the Apostles.

Four lost pages (pp. [109–112]=8 columns=256 lines)

One codex sheet with 256 lines is missing following 13:18 (= p. [108]), and for which the scribe's pagination would have been 109–112 (see Introduction). When the text resumes at 14:1 (= p. [113]), there is a change from the voice of the narrator and the passion theme, to the voice of the apostles and the narration of their second extant visionary account.

14:1–24: Apostles' vision remnant two (p. 113.1–114.64)

The text resumes with the conclusion of a sentence (14:1), followed by the scribe's colon signaling the end of a sense unit, but the identity of the speaker is unclear. The narrative voice that commences is that of the apostles, who now describe their second vision. The description extends across four columns of text and into the lacuna after 14:24. The first complete sentence begins with the correlative adverb of time "then" (τότε), introducing a new sense unit with an em-

---

98. Cf. 1 Enoch 48:1–2; 4 Ezra 14:38–41; OdesSol 11:6–13; GThom 13, (35,4b–7a); 108 (50,28–30); GkAcThom 47.
99. Cf. Rev 1:7.
100. Cf. John 19:34.
101. Cf. John 19:35; 21:24.

phatic reference to the apostles (14:2), perhaps indicating a change of subject from that of the preceding sentence. The title "apostles" is used only here in this gospel (cf. line 12). Their comment that "this world became as the darkness" is paralleled in apocalyptic texts in which the world, or lower heavens appear as darkness, or as nothing in relation to the higher brighter heavens, and often at the beginning of an ascent.[102]

A description of the apostles' transformation follows (14:3; cf. 7:1–2). Their transformed bodies are described in relation to a group called, "[those] among the Aeons [of glory],"[103] a reference to either angels (ubiquitous in ascent texts), or sanctified ancients in transformed states, such as Moses and Elijah.[104]

They then describe an experience in which they were invested with "[our] apostleship" (14:4), thus basing apostolic authority on visionary experience[105] and ecstatic ascent,[106] in contrast to the earthly investitures described elsewhere.[107] The Strasbourg Papyrus mentions "apostleship," with the visionary image of being "clothed" with the power of apostleship (cf. 14:9).[108] Such apostolic investitures appear to have developed from the priestly and related investitures in Jewish apocalypses, ultimately deriving from Exodus 28. It is unknown who invests apostleship in the Gospel of the Savior (cf. p. 113.10–12). In their ascents, Levi receives the heavenly garments of the priesthood from seven angels,[109] Enoch receives his heavenly robes and crown from "the Holy One" (i.e., God),[110] while the apostles in the Strasbourg Papyrus are "clothed" with the power of apostleship by an unidentified figure, presumably the glorified Jesus.[111] The apostles then witness the Savior after he attained the fourth heaven (14:5),[112] indicating either that they were not invested by him, or that he ascended to the fourth heaven after investing them in the third heaven.[113] It is not clear how many heavens are in the author's cosmology. The noun "disturbance," followed by a period, suggests the end of a lost sentence (line 23).

When the text resumes in 14:6, the apostles are narrating their vision. They describe the angels and the archangels fleeing,[114] as in the first vision (7:5), but here their destination is apparently the presence of the Cherubim (14:7). The

---

102. Cf. AscenIs 8:21; TLevi 3:1–2; 1 Enoch 17:2 (Gk Akhmim ms); 2 Enoch 7:1 (ms J); ApocZeph 2:6–7; GkApocPaul 13 (Schneemelcher and Wilson, 2.720); DSav 122, 1b–123,4.
103. Cf. Zost 5,15–17a.
104. Cf. Mark 9:2–4; GkApocPet 16–17 (Eth); cf. 4–20 (Gk) (Schneemelcher and Wilson, 2.633–35).
105. Cf. Gal 1:15–16; Acts 9:3–9; 22:6–11; 26:12–18.
106. Cf. 2 Cor 12:1–5.
107. Cf. Matt 10:1–4; Luke 6:13–15.
108. Cf. Copt. 6, recto and verso, pp. 157–58.
109. Cf. TLevi 8:1–10.
110. Cf. 3 Enoch 12:1–5.
111. Cf. Copt. 6, verso, p. 158.
112. Cf. John 6:62.
113. Cf. 2 Cor 12:2.
114. Cf. Zost 4,25b–31a.

Cherubim inhabit the heavenly throne room in early Jewish and Christian angelology, and are often mentioned as a visionary ascends to the throne room,[115] suggesting that this vision concerns the throne room (cf. 14:8–9). The reconstructed phrase in line 31 may reflect Ezekiel's description of the unusual movements of the Cherubim and other angelic creatures, where they are described as moving in various directions, but not downward.[116]

The apostles' description continues in 14:8–9, with descriptions of two activities in the throne room. In the first, an unidentified group cast down their crowns[117] in front of the Father's throne, reminiscent of the 24 elders (i.e., presbyters [πρεσβύτερος]) of Rev 4:2–10. Although damage to the manuscript prevents certainty in any further textual reconstruction, the fragmentary remains of the Greek words "to hymn (ὑμνεῖν)" (cf. frg. 9F.39), or the nominal "hymn (ὕμνος)," and "elder" (πρεσβύτερος), possibly can be identified in lines 35 and 36 (e.g., ϩγμν[ος . . . ⲡⲣⲉ]/ⲥⲃⲩⲧⲉⲣ[ⲟⲥ), indicating the singing of hymns, perhaps by or near the elders.[118] Immediately prior to the parallel Gethsemane prayer in Matt 26:36–44, Jesus and the disciples also sing a hymn.[119] This raises the possibility that the author of the Gospel of the Savior makes a visionary reinterpretation of the Matthean passage, so that the hymn singing by Jesus and the disciples before their departure for Gethsemane is here associated with the roughly coterminous singing of hymns in the throne room. In both cases, hymn singing precedes the Son's prayer to the Father.

The second activity in the throne room appears to be a reward ceremony involving the reception of robes by "all the holy ones" (14:9), reminiscent of the martyrs who receive white robes in Rev 6:9–11 (see comments on "the garment of the kingdom," 1:6).

In early Jewish and Christian visionary ascent texts, such ecstastic ascents to the throne room, complete with Cherubim, hymn singing, and reward scenes involving crowns and robes, are preparatory to a more climactic event. The ascended visionary then enters the throne room and falls down before the enthroned Father to pray or receive further revelation, often including dialogue with angels or God himself.[120] In the following prayer of the Son to the Father, the author of the Gospel of the Savior provides a visionary reinterpretation of the Gethsemane prayer of Jesus similar to that in Matt 26:36–46. Whereas Matthew shows the apostles sleeping,[121] the author of the Gospel of the Savior

---

115. Cf. 1 Kgs 22:19; Isa 6:1–2; Ezek 1:4–2:1; 10:1–22; 1 Enoch 14:12; 3 Enoch 6:2; 7:1; Rev 4:2–11.

116. Cf. Ezek 1:9–21; 10:15–19; 1 Enoch 14:23.

117. Cf. Isa 28:5; 62:3; WisSol 5:16; 1 Cor 9:25; 2 Tim 4:8; Jas 1:12; 1 Pet 5:4; Rev 2:10b; 3:11b.

118. Cf. Rev 4:10–11; 5:8–10; 7:11–12; 11:16–18; 14:3.

119. Cf. Matt 26:30: "and when they had sung a hymn (ὑμνεῖν). . . . "

120. Cf. Isa 6; 1 Enoch 14:8–15:1; 2 Enoch 21; TLevi 5:1–2; 8:1–19; AscenIs 9:6–18, 24–26; ApocPaul 22,23a–24,8.

121. Cf. Matt 26:40, 43, 45.

possibly reveals that, although their bodies are asleep in Gethsemane, they, like Enoch,[122] are not sleeping, but are ascended in spirit, observing the ascended Savior's intercessory prayer in the throne room.

The next three columns of text (pp. 113.44–114.64) are heavily damaged, yet the interpretation offered here has the advantage of providing a plausible and coherent explanation of five technical details: (1) a general sense for the two words "after" (ⲚⲦⲈⲢⲈ̣[; 14:10) and, possibly, "Son" (ϢⲎⲢ̣[Ⲉ; 14:10), (2) the correct sequence for each of the two temporal adverbs "after" (ⲚⲦⲈⲢⲈ̣[; 14:10), and "again" (ⲞⲚ; 14:17), (3) the correct ordinal sequences for the two phrases "the second time" ([ⲠⲘⲈϨⲤ]ⲈⲠ ⲤⲚ̣ⲀⲨ; 14:24), and "the third time" (ⲠⲘⲈϨϢⲞ̣[ⲘⲚ̄Ⲧ] Ⲛ̄ⲤⲞⲠ; p. 115.30–31a), (4) the antecedent for the pronominal prefix "he" (ϥ-) (14:12), and (5) the antecedent for the pronominal prefix in the conjunctive "and you (sg.)" (Ⲛ̄Ⲅ-) (14:24).

The editor apparently introduces a new scene "after" the reward scene, in which the "Son" is prostrate before the enthroned Father for the first time (14:10; see comments on 14:17, where he later prostrates himself "again"). The use of the christological title "Son" is limited in this gospel to this scene (cf. 14:10, 17, 24; p. 115.29) and apparently derives from one of the author's sources for this prayer of the "Son" to the Father.[123] Beyond the context of the prayer, the word "son" is apparently insignificant to the author, who otherwise uses the titles "Savior" and "Lord." The two other uses of "son" are either neutral ("child" in 13:2), or involve an unrelated christological tradition of royal sonship (13:8).

The following question (14:11), presumably from the enthroned Father (cf. 14:8),[124] indicates that the Son was "weeping and [distressed],"[125] and that has disturbed the angels who had possibly fled to the Cherubim in the throne room (cf. 14:6–7). Such questions appear in a variety of apocalyptic texts where an elder or an angelic guide inquires into the emotional distress of the visionary.[126] It is not clear if the Son prays in the lost text in lines 46–52, or only weeps with distress, as a prelude to his prayers in the next two columns (cf. 14:13–15, 17b–23).

The narrator then introduces the Savior as the next speaker (14:12), but the first five lines of his reply are missing (lines 60–64). When the text resumes at 14:13, the Son is apparently still speaking in response to the question about his distress. This section has at least three sayings. The first saying (14:13) indicates that the Savior's distress concerns the fate of "the people (*λαός*) [of] Israel"(cf. 14:11).[127]

122. Cf. 1 Enoch 13:10; 14:2.

123. Cf. "my Father" in Matt 26:39, 42; cf. John 17:1.

124. Cf. 1 Kgs 22:19–23; Ezek 1:28b–2:2.

125. Cf. Heb 5:7–8; Matt 26:37b–38a; Mark 14:33b–34a; Luke 22:43–44; John 12:27–30.

126. Cf. 1 Enoch 21:9–10; 83:3–6; GkApocPaul 33 (Schneemelcher and Wilson, 2.731).

127. Cf. Luke 21:24, where the subject is Jerusalem's fate and the "wrath (*ὀργή*) against this people (*λαός*)."

The second saying (14:14) begins with an address to the Father, indicating that his reply to the Father's question has concluded, and that his prayer has begun with a plea that the "cup" he must drink might pass by him, a metaphor for his death on the cross.[128] The saying is nearly identical to the Coptic version of Matt 26:39,[129] but with the addition of the exclamatory address "O," and a synonym for "cup" (ϫⲱ in Matthew; ⲁⲡⲟⲧ in Gospel of the Savior), possibly evidencing the author or translator is again under continued influence of the Gospel of Matthew in Coptic.

The third saying (14:15) refers back to "the people of Israel" (lines 5b–6a; cf. 13b), indicating that Israel's fate, and not that of the apostles, as in John 17:6–19, nor his own fate, as in Matt 26:38–44, is the central request of the prayer. In other texts, Jesus is also portrayed as an intercessor for Israel or the world,[130] as are a variety of other heavenly beings.[131]

When the text resumes after a lacuna of eight lines (lines 14–21a), the identity of the speaker is unclear for 14:16, but it appears to be the narrator, in a statement similar to a saying of Jesus in Luke 19:9,[132] and possibly suggests that salvation, however defined, was granted to Israel and the world as the successful result of the Savior's intercession. It is unlikely that it is spoken by the Father, despite similar statements by him in other texts,[133] because the later statement at 14:24 seems to be the Father's next, or second comment, in relation to his first (14:11). The scribe's colon and dash in line 23b indicate the end of the sense unit.

The narrator again introduces the next speaker as "the Son," who "again" (i.e., for the second time; see comments on 14:10) kneels before the Father (14:17).[134] This narration is paralleled in Matt 26:39 and 26:42, where the Savior also prays a second and a third time before the betrayal scene. The influence of a Coptic version of Matt 26:39 is suggested by the forms ⲡⲁϩⲧϥ̄ ("he bowed"), ⲉϫⲛ̄ ("upon"), ⲉϥϫⲱ ⲙⲙⲟⲥ (the verb "saying"), and the reference to the "cup," rather than the "hour" of Mark 14:35.[135] Saying 14:17 has the Savior bowing upon his "knees" (ⲡⲁⲧ), in agreement with Coptic Luke 22:41,[136] and contrary to Mark 14:35, which has him bow "upon the earth,"

---

128. Cf. Matt 26:39; cf. John 18:11.
129. And not Mark 14:36 or Luke 22:42.
130. Cf. Rom 8:32–34; ApJas 11,4b–6a; Strasbourg Papyrus, Copt. 5, recto.
131. Cf. 1 Enoch 15:2; 40:6; 89:76; 90:14; TLevi 5:6; Rom 8:26–27; 11:2; Heb 7:25.
132. Cf. Rom 11:11–12.
133. Cf. Isa 49:6; Acts 13:47; Rev 12:10.
134. Cf. 1 Enoch 14:14b, 24–25; ApocAb 10:2–3; 17:2–5.
135. On the Coptic word ⲟⲛ ("again"), see the Coptic texts from the same scenes in Matt 26:42 and Mark 14:39.
136. Agreements between the Gospel of the Savior and the Gospel of Luke are rare, but do demonstrate the influence of traditions also attested in Luke on the author of the Gospel of the Savior; cf. comments on 1:3.

and Matt 26:39, which has him bow "upon his face." The Savior then prays another intercessory prayer for Israel (14:17b–24), but the first five lines are mostly lost.

In saying 14:18, he notes his resolve to die with joy and shed his blood (cf. 1:6b), indicating the arrest has not yet occurred, and that the Savior, or at least his body of flesh, is expected to die. The image of pouring out blood, previously referred to as "the blood of the grape," a eucharistic image for wine (see comments at 1:6), is equally attested in Matt 26:28 and Mark 14:24. They also both have "for many" (ϩⲁ ϩⲁϩ), contrary to GSav 14:18, which has "for the human race," suggesting the author views the Savior's death as a blood sacrifice on behalf of others. This is similar to the sayings on self-sacrifice on behalf of others in GSav 4:8–12.

In saying 14:19, he does not relate his weeping to his own danger, but to his concern over the ability of Israel (i.e., the seed of "Abraham, Isaac, and Jacob"[137]) to "stand" in the judgment.[138] In saying 14:20, he notes that he will sit on his throne and judge the world.

The partially preserved saying 14:21 is reminiscent of the apocalyptic judgement scene in Matt 25:31–46, where two groups respond to the Savior in their own defense. If the word "[to] me" (ⲛ]ⲁⲓ̈) can be reconstructed in line 53 of saying 14:22, its occurrence also in line 48 suggests that there are responses from two groups to the Savior as judge, as in Matt 25:37 and 44, indicating that the saying possibly extends at least to line 53, and might have been a shorter version of the traditions found in Matt 25:31–46.[139] The saying's opening phrase, "They will say to me, that . . . " (lines 47b–48), is paralleled with five occurrences in Matt 25:34–45, where such transitional comments occur in a story attributed to Jesus in order to introduce the story's various speakers (e.g., "Then they also will answer, that . . . " in Matt 25:44).[140] The rest of the saying mentions his glorification "on earth"[141] as a past event; the reference is obscure, but it possibly refers to the revelation of his glory previously discussed with the apostles (cf. 12:1–10), or his future crucifixion. The Son then apparently concludes his prayer with a plea that something pass by him, presumably the cup that he must drink.

Lines 62–64 are heavily damaged, but the ordinal reference to "the second time," and the second-person masculine singular "and you (sg.)," suggest the possibility that the Father addresses the Son for a second time. A conjectural reconstruction of the text in line 62a can be made following the author's style,

137. Cf. Matt 8:11; 22:32; Luke 13:28; 20:37.
138. Cf. Rom 9:27–28.
139. Cf. Matt 7:22; Luke 13:27.
140. Cf. Matt 25:34, 37, 40, 44, 45.
141. Cf. John 17:4–5.

[πἴωτ πεϫαϥ] ["The Father said"] (cf. Coptic text for 6:2a), but [πεϫε πἴωτ] is also possible. If the text is reconstructed following a similar phrase in the Coptic version of John 21:16 (πεϫαϥ ον ναϥ ⲙ̄πμεϩⲥⲛ̄ ⲥⲛⲁⲩ ϫε), "he said again to him the second time," the reader would be required to understand the identity of the speaker (i.e., the Father in 14:24) from the context.

Concerning the lacuna in line 64a, the conjunctive ⲛ̄ⲅ- at the end of the line requires a preceding verb, so a reconstruction of the first phrase with an imperative, often accompanying the conjunctive, might look like this [ϫε ⲁⲩ] ⲡⲁ̣ϣ̣ⲏⲣⲉ "Come, my Son," or [ϫε ϫⲣ]ⲟ̣ ⲡϣ̣ⲏⲣⲉ "Be strong, Son," resulting in the following conjectural reconstruction of lines 62b–64, "The Father said to him for the second time, 'Come, my Son, and you . . . ,'" but the rest of the Father's statement is lost with the missing upper portion of the next page. The text which can be placed at the furthest point in the page order is p. 114.64.

Fragments 4–27: basic issues

The original location of each of the remaining fragments (frgs. 4–27) in relation to fragments 1–3 is unknown, though they all appear to be related on the basis of the same scribal hand, writing materials, and content. There is no evidence that any of the remaining fragments do or do not come from another codex similarly constructed and inscribed by the same scribe, or from another text in the same codex.[142] In approaching this problem, one recognizes the general paucity of useful data among the remaining fragments that otherwise could be employed to argue for or against any particular fragment as a part of the Gospel of the Savior. Note, for example, the fragments with little or no text,[143] or those fragments with text that can be argued to reflect the style, terminology, and type of traditional materials employed in the Gospel of the Savior, even though they may belong to another text from the same codex.[144] Only a few fragments will be regarded as almost certainly belonging to the Gospel of the Savior.[145] One is encouraged to think that they were all originally related in some fashion, and were possibly from the same composition, because the original locations of some of the smaller fragments already have been identified among the larger fragments (see Introduction). Given these interpretive problems, the commentary will discuss the remaining fragments primarily in relation to each other and to the extant text of the Gospel of the Savior with its related literature, as presented in the preceding commentary for fragments 1–3.

142. E.g., Nag Hammadi Codex II, where several similar texts were copied into one book.

143. See frgs. 6F/H, 10H, 12F/H, 13F/H, 15F/H, 17F, 18F/H, 24F, 25F, 26F/H, 27F/H.

144. See frgs. 4F/H, 5F/H, 7F/H, 9F/H, 10F, 11F/H, 14F/H, 17H, 19F/H, 20F/H, 21F/H, 22F/H, 23F/H, 24H, 25H.

145. See frgs. 5F/H and 9H.

Fragment 4

Fragment 4 is the lower portion of a bifolium with the partial remains of four pages. As noted in the Introduction, the page numbers for frg. 4 are assigned for convenience. Beginning with p. 115, a narrator's introduction appears in which the Son is introduced and prays to the Father for "the third time" (p. 115.29–31a; cf. 14:17).[146] If p. 115.29–32 is a continuation of the visionary throne scene in 14:8–24, then the Son prays at least three times before the Father.[147] It also indicates that what appears to be the Father's lost statement to the Son, initiated at 14:24b, possibly occupied most of p. 115. After the Son's characteristic address, "O, My [Father]," the fragmentary sentence in line 32b begins midsentence with ⲉϣⲭⲉ ("if," "indeed," "then"), similar to one of the Son's previous prayers (14:14), but the fragmentary sentence at p. 115 cannot be restored.

After a loss of 93 lines, the text resumes on p. 116.29–32 with a reference to completing "the service" (λειτουργία). It is not clear whether this statement is spoken by a character from the Gospel of the Savior, or is one of it's narrator's comments (cf. 12:18), or is from another composition copied by the same scribe. Of interest is the Greek word λειτουργία, which has a broad range in early Christian usage. The simple use of the term refers to an individual's "service" performed for the state, but in theological discussions it refers to religious service, especially that of priests in a temple,[148] or religious service among Christians,[149] while the verb (λειτουργεῖν) can refer to the heavenly service of angels in the throne room.[150] This range of options indicates that this obscure reference to "service" can only be discussed in terms of its numerous possibilities.

Legible text resumes on p. 121, lines 28–32, after a loss of at least four complete pages. The identity of the prophet is unknown; if the element ⲛ̄ϭⲓ ("namely")[151] can be restored in line 29, the lost prophet's name might have originally followed in the four or five letter spaces remaining in line 29b. If the following saying is a quote from the unidentified prophet, this is the second time the author refers to the authority of a prophetic quote (cf. 4:7). However, if a period was lost in the lacuna after the word "prophet," then the following phrase "[he] said to us," was not part of the same sentence. This allows the possibility that the word "prophet" was part of a preceding comment or question from the apostles, followed by the narrator's comment beginning a new sentence, "He said to us," in which case the speaker of the following saying is not

146. Cf. Matt 26:44; Mark 14:41; Luke 23:22; John 21:17.
147. Cf. once in John 17 and Luke 22; twice in Mark 14; and thrice in Matt 26.
148. Cf. Exod 38:21 (= LXX: 37:19); Luke 1:23; Heb 8:6.
149. Cf. Phil 2:30; 1 Clem 44:2.
150. Cf. TLevi 3:5; 1 Clem 34:5–6.
151. The element is employed to introduce subjects and is often untranslated.

the prophet. This is further indicated by the fact that the supposed quote cannot be identified as having come from any of the traditional biblical prophets.

The author employs a quotation formula (lines 27b–30a) in which the identity of the speaker (cf. "us," line 29) cannot be determined, although the plural suggests the narrating apostles from the Gospel of the Savior. This introduces what appears to be a two stich saying in synonymous parallelism, where "lot" and "glory" are equated. The reference to "glory" can possibly be related to the theology of glory exhibited in the Gospel of the Savior (cf. 12:4; 14:3, 22), suggesting that their "lot" is eschatological,[152] or possibly even ecstatic.[153] The next legible text in line 62 is found with the word "wood," which can possibly be restored to ⲡϣⲉ ⲙ̄[ⲡⲉⲥ̄ⲣ̄ⲟ̄ⲥ̄] ("the wood of [the cross]"), raising the possibility of a reference to the crucifixion, but it cannot be determined whether the crucifixion occurs at this point in the story.

The text resumes on p. 122.1–3, where only a few letters and two words ("strength" and "kingdom") are visible, and lines 31–32, where the word "shadow" is possibly in reference to the cross, mentioned four lines later, similar to its use in 9:2 (cf. frg. 21F.2–3). The text continues at the top of the next column (21F.35) with an address, possibly to the cross. The address beginning with "O," a characteristic speech device of the Savior, indicates this portion of text is possibly from the Gospel of the Savior; although "O, Entirety" remains obscure, it might be a reference to the Pleroma (cf. frg. 5F.32) from a gnostic perspective. When legible text resumes in line 54 the cross is still a topic.

At lines 60–64, the identification of the speaker is unknown, but it could be understood as the Savior, who already has taken the apostles (cf. "you [pl.]") to heaven with him in at least two previous ascents in the Gospel of the Savior (7:1–7; 14:1–5). In this case, it would be at least their third ascent to heaven with him. The reference to teaching in heaven suggests visionary ascent in which revelations are given to the apostles. If the speaker is the Savior, the reference to "three days" possibly indicates the conclusion of a passion prediction (cf. "cross" in lines 35 and 54), but with an ecstatic ascent to heaven with the apostles, rather than a single body rising from the dead.[154] However, the Markan phrase, "after three days" (ⲙⲛ̄ⲛ̄ⲥⲁ ϣⲟⲙⲛ̄ⲧ ⲛ̄ϩⲟⲟⲩ) requires the word "after" (ⲙⲛ̄ⲛ̄ⲥⲁ), which is too large for the lacuna in line 60a. But, the lost text in line 60a can also be reconstructed with an ordinal number, "the third," [ⲡⲙⲉϩϣ]ⲟⲙⲛ̄ⲧ, as in the shared formula employed by Matt and Luke, "he will rise on the third day" (ⲛ̄ϥ̄ⲧⲱⲟⲩⲛ ϩⲙ̄ ⲡⲙⲉϩϣⲟⲙⲛ̄ⲧ ⲛ̄ϩⲟⲟⲩ), but the extant letters in line 59b do not easily conform to the first part of that formula.[155] If the

152. Cf. κλῆρος in Acts 26:18; Col 1:12; IgnEph 11:2; IgnRom 1:2; IgnTr 12:3; IgnPhd 5:1; TriTrac 89,34; OrWorld 114,20b–21.

153. Cf. κλῆρος in 1 ApocJas 29,9–17.

154. Cf. Mark 8:31; 9:31; 10:34.

155. Cf. Matt 16:21; 17:23; 20:19; Luke 9:22; 18:33; 24:7, 21, 46.

words are not part of a passion prediction, they may be spoken to the disciples by the Savior on the day of the crucifixion, or even while he is nailed to the cross (see comments on GSav p. 121.62), and thus are similar to his promise to the crucified criminal that he will be in paradise with him "today."[156] The period of three days could also indicate a three day period in Hades (see comments on 2:1), after which the ascent will occur. The promised tour of heaven, in which teaching takes place, is a common theme in Jewish and Christian apocalypses,[157] and might provide the context for the events, apparently a tour of heaven, described in frgs. 14F.22–31; 14H.19–31; 19H.2–6 and 19F.2–7.

Fragment 5

Fragment 5H/F is the lower portion of a single leaf, possibly to be identified as the lower portion of p. [105] and p. [106] (see Introduction). In this case, the extant text would be part of the Savior's speech on those pages. Thus, we begin with the hair side of the fragment.

The speaker of the two words in frg. 5H.23–24 is unknown. The second person singular ("you") is spoken in the Gospel of the Savior by the apostles when addressing the Savior, by the Savior when addressing the cross and possibly by the Father when addressing the Son (p. 114.64). The "Amen" is spoken only by the Savior in the Gospel of the Savior, supporting the suggestion that frg. 5H is the bottom portion of p. [105], where the Savior appears to be the speaker.

The text resumes in line 51 with the first saying (lines 51–53). Although it is not certain that the words in lines 51–52 are part of the same sentence, they occur together in reference to the order of resurrection in Acts 26:23 and 1 Thess 4:16 (cf. frg. 5F.27–29). The address, "O cross," appears to be the concluding refrain of the saying (cf. frg. 5H.57 and 63), indicating that the Savior is the speaker of this first saying. This supports the suggestion that lines 51–64 comprise the bottom portion of the missing right-hand column of p. [105] (i.e. frg. 5F.33–50), where the Savior also addresses the cross with similar sayings, each possibly followed by the same refrain, "O cross."

The second saying (lines 53b–57) is also directed to the cross ("you [sg.]") and refers to an exaltation, which is the wish or desire of the cross, perhaps a poetic reference to the physical raising of the cross for the crucifixion. The saying also concludes with the refrain addressing the cross.

The third saying (line 58a) is an injunction to the cross not to be afraid, apparently because the Savior is rich[158] and will fill the cross with his wealth, as in the fourth saying (lines 58b–61a; cf. the same saying in frg. 5F.19b–22). The "wealth" is a reference to the Power and Spirit of God,[159] which resides in mor-

---

156. Cf. Luke 23:43.
157. Cf. 2 Enoch 8; 3 Enoch 11:3; GkApocPaul 19–30, 45–51.
158. Cf. 2 ApocJas 47,7b–8a.
159 Cf. GThom 85; Justin, 1 Apol 33:6; GThom 106,21–28; Acts 8:9–24.

tals as wealth in poverty.[160] The fifth saying (lines 61b–63) reflects the Savior's resolute eagerness for the cross (cf. 11:2), similar to that of Andrew in the Acts of Andrew,[161] and concludes with the refrain addressing the cross. The sixth saying (line 64) is extant only in its first part and remains obscure.

The text on the other side (the flesh side of the fragment)[162] is comprised of four sayings, presumably by the Savior and addressed to the cross. The last three sayings are each introduced by a recurring phrase in which the cross is addressed ("A little longer, O cross"), indicating this is a poetic section, perhaps a hymn to the cross.

Each of the sayings juxtaposes opposite states of being through the use of opposite images, the first valued negatively, the second positively. The terms and usage employed here are common in gnostic texts, where (assuming a cosmic myth of the pre-mundane fall) the entire spiritual universe (Pleroma) is restored. Thus, "poverty" will be filled with "wealth;" that which is "lacking" will be "perfected;" that which is "diminished" will be "full;" that which "fell arises;" and "all the pleroma is perfected."[163] The gnostic Treatise on the Resurrection describes such images as "the symbols and images of the resurrection" in spirit, not in the physical body (48,38–49,5). These images provide the strongest evidence for the gnostic proclivity of the passage, and possibly for all of the Gospel of the Savior as well (see comments on 4:1).

The first saying (5F.19–22) begins midsentence and is attested nearby at 5H.58b–61a. The second-person singular apparently refers to the cross, as in 5H.58b–61a. The initial adversative conjunction "but" (ἀλλά) possibly indicates a contrast between an image of poverty (representing the Spirit's absence), now lost in the preceding phrase, and wealth (representing the Spirit's presence).

The second saying (5F.23–26) begins with the refrain addressed to the cross. On the phrase, "[A little longer]" see comments on 13:3. As noted above, the saying continues with a two stich construction in synonymous parallelism, contrasting opposite states of being. The change from future tense orientation in the first saying, to present tense orientation in the second through fourth sayings, possibly suggests the reconstitution of the Pleroma already is effected through the work of the Savior and the ecstatic experiences of the apostles.

The third saying (5F.27–29) also begins with the refrain addressed to the cross and continues with a simple statement employing an image of falling and rising. The saying is attested as a saying of the resurrected Jesus in the orthodox Epistula Apostolorum, where it refers to the death of any individual believer, whose physical body will be resurrected with the soul ("what has fallen will

---

160. Cf. GThom 29.
161. Cf. AcAndrew p. 349 (Schneemelcher and Wilson, 2.148).
162. Frg. 5F.19–32.
163. Cf. ApJas 2,23–4,22; DSav 139,13b–20a; TreatRes 48,38–49,5; GTruth 21,14–18; 24,21–25,3; GEgypt 59,10–18; GPhil 85,31–32; 86,13–14.

arise," and "the flesh will rise alive with the soul," cf. EpApos 25–26). This suggests the third saying is interpreted in the Gospel of the Savior according to gnostic conceptualizations, so that the present ecstatic experience of the Savior and other humans is participatory in the eschatological restoration of the Pleroma.

The fourth saying (5F.30–32) also begins with the refrain addressed to the cross and continues with a comment that "all the Pleroma is perfected." The following lines are lost, so it is unclear whether this is the first stich of a two part saying, is followed by more sayings, or is the final saying in a series culminating in a statement about the perfection of the Pleroma.[164]

Fragments with upper margins

Fragment 6 Fragment 6 is a remnant of a leaf with the top edge and upper margin extant on both sides. 6H.1 has one line and one reconstructed word ("upon").

Fragment 7 Fragment 7 is the top central portion of a leaf with the upper margin, the center margin, and the top five lines of two columns on both sides. In 7H.33, one of numerous Greek words beginning with οἰκο (e.g., οἶκος "house," or, οἰκομένη "the inhabited world") possibly begins line 1, and the abbreviation for "cross" (ⲤⲢⲟ̄Ⲥ) is probably found in line 36. In 7F.3, the abbreviation for "cross" can perhaps be reconstructed with the definite article, ⲡⲉⲥ̄]ⲣ̄ⲟ[Ⲥ. The word "cross" is only spoken by the Savior in the Gospel of the Savior (in those places where the speaker can be identified), suggesting the Savior speaks here as well. This fragment might be related to fragment 5 which also has addresses to the cross on both sides of a single leaf (frg. 5H.53,57,63; 5F.23,28,31; cf. frg. 11F and 11H).

Fragments with double columns and center margin only

Fragment 9 Fragment 9 is the central portion of a leaf with the center margin intact and parts of both columns on both sides. 9F.3 has the Greek word "wisdom" (σοφία), occuring only here among the fragments. On "the wood" (line 4), see p. 121.62. 9F.39 has the Greek word "to hymn" (ὑμνεῖν) (see comments on 14:8–9). 9H.37 has the Greek word "prophet" (προφήτης) in either singular or plural form (see comments on 4:7). A conjectural reconstruction of (9H.38–39) is ⲁⲃⲣⲁ[ϩⲁⲙ ⲙⲛ̄ⲓ̄ⲥⲁ]/ⲁⲕ [ⲙⲛ̄ⲓ̄ⲁⲕⲱⲃ] (cf. 14:19). Lines 9H.2b–3a conclude a narrative comment by the apostles and an editorial transitional phrase introducing the new speaker (9H.3b), presumably the Savior, who speaks in his characteristic phrasing, "O, my holy members" (see comments on 6:1–2). The saying which follows is a macarism (cf. 1:3) concerning the apostles' blessed status, apparently due to an action which "this one" (the Savior? God the Father?) has performed on their behalf.

---

164. Cf. GSav p. 122.32; TreatRes 48,38b–49,5.

Fragment 10 Fragment 10 is the central portion of a leaf with the center margin intact and parts of both columns on both sides. 10F.4 has the word "to you (sg.)," suggesting the apostles speaking to the Savior, or the Savior speaking to the cross. 10F.33 possibly has the word "Amen," again suggesting the Savior as speaker. 10F.34 possibly has the name "Jacob" (ⲓⲁⲕⲱⲃ), but a conjectural reconstruction suggests "James" (ⲓⲁⲕⲱⲃ[ⲟⲥ]; cf. 14:19 and comments on 9H.37–39). Line 10F.35 begins with the letters ⲥⲏⲥ, possibly the name "Moses" ([ⲙⲱ ÿ]ⲥⲏⲥ).

Fragments with bottom margins

Fragment 11 Fragment 11 is the lower portion of a leaf with a single column and bottom margin intact on both sides. Fragment 11F.31–32 can be compared to 12:7–10.

Fragment 12 Fragment 12 is the lower portion of a leaf with a single column and bottom margin intact on both sides. The single word "be firm" ⲧⲁ ⲭⲣⲏⲩ (12H.31), occurs in gospel texts at Matt 7:25 and Luke 16:26.

Fragment 13 Fragment 13 is the lower portion of a leaf, with traces of the last line of a column, and the bottom margin intact on both sides. No complete words are visible.

Fragment with a side, or center margin and a bottom margin

Fragment 14 Fragment 14 is reconstructed from three fragments that were originally separated. It is a portion of a leaf with the bottom margin and a left margin intact on one side, and a right margin on the other. In both cases, the margin could be the center margin of its page. Text on both sides of the fragment indicate a dialogue, possibly between the apostles and the Savior, or an angelic guide, while walking through the heavenly Jerusalem (14F.22–31 and 14H.19–31). A dialogue between the Savior and the apostles, while walking through the earthly Jerusalem cannot be ruled out (cf. Matt 24:1; Mark 13:1–2), but this is unlikely, considering the apostles do not know the name of the city (14F.23b–27a), an ignorance that would better be explained if they were somewhere else than the earthly Jerusalem.

The text opens with the conclusion of a sentence concerning "that city," but the identity of the speaker is unknown (14F.22b–23a). A narrator's comment comes from the spokesperson for the apostles, who asks the name of the city (14F.23b–25a). Another narrator's comment introduces the Savior, or an angelic guide as the next speaker, who identifies the city as Jerusalem (14F.25b–27a).[165] Similar scenes are found in early Jewish and Christian apocalyptic texts, where ascended visionaries like Zephaniah or Paul are shown scenes in and around the heavenly Jerusalem, while they ask questions of their

---

165. Cf. Rev 21:1–22:5.

angelic guides.166 In a text parallel to 14F.19–31, Paul asks his guiding angel, while in the midst of a tour of the city, "Who, sir, is this here with such great power?" and the response is, "This is David. This is the City of Jerusalem."167 The apparent tour of heaven may be related to the promise of a tour of heaven on p. 122.60b–63a, though it is not clear when the tour takes place in relation to the story.

Fragment 14H.19–31 contains text similar to that in 14F.22b–27a, so possibly is part of the tour of heaven. Fragment 14H.24–26 evidences the apostles asking a question about "this place," followed by a response ("he said" 14H.28), presumably from the Savior.

Fragment with centerfold

Fragment 15 Fragment 15 is a portion of a codex sheet, with a centerfold (cf. frgs. 1, 2, and 4), with the remains of four pages; but, only a few letters and no complete words are visible.

Fragment containing mostly center margin

Fragment 16 Fragment 16 is mostly the center margin between two columns, with a few individual letter traces on both sides; no words.

Fragments with side or center margin

Fragment 17 Fragment 17 is a portion of a leaf, in about the center of a column, with seven lines per side. 17F has a right margin and 17H a left margin. It is not certain whether the extant margins are the center, inner or outer margins of their pages. 17F.5 has the only occurrence among the fragments of the Greek term "righteous," ($\delta\iota\kappa\alpha\iota\sigma$). 17H.4–6 contains a phrase, but the speaker is unknown, possibly an apostle, or the Father. The words are directed to an unidentified person (cf. "your [sg.]"), apparently the Savior. The image suggests an eschatological enthronement scene, rather than one associated with an ecstatic visionary ascent. Similar orthodox texts are employed in reference to the apocalyptic exaltation and enthronement of the Son, sitting at the right hand of the Father, often including judgment of the world.168

Fragment 18 Fragment 18 is a portion of a leaf, with no margins visible on 18F, but 18H has a right margin along three lines of text. It is not certain whether the extant margin is the center, inner or outer margin of its page. The presence of the word "hand," suggests a possible relation to "foot," in 7:7.

166. Cf. ApocZeph 2,5; ApocPaul 18,13b–23; GkApocPaul 22–30 (Schneemelcher and Wilson, 2.726–30).

167. GkApocPaul 29 (Schneemelcher and Wilson, 2.729); cf. AcPet12Apos 1.30–2.4; 6:19–7.5; EpApos 1.30–2.4; 6.19–7.5.

168. Cf. Psa 110:1; Matt 25:31–33; 26:64; Mark 16:19; Acts 2:34; Rom 8:34; Col 3:1; Heb 1:3; 8:1; 12:2; 1 Pet 3:22; ApJas 14,30.

Both words occur in close proximity, and in an apocalyptic saying concerning bodily transformation, in GThom saying 22.

Fragments (large) from center of a column, in a series of nearly identical shapes

Fragment 19 Fragment 19 is a portion of a column with right and left margins visible on the flesh side, and a left margin on the hair side. 19H.2–6 suggest a scene in a tour of heaven (cf. p. 122.60–63a), where one or more rivers of milk and honey run near or through the heavenly Jerusalem.[169] The antecedent of the feminine singular pronominal prefix cannot be the expected "river" (masc sg), as in GkApocPaul 22–23,31, but is possibly one or two springs, like the "spring [fem] of the water of life" (see comments on 13:16).

Fragment 19F.2–7 is reminiscent of the curse in Psa 109:9–15. The curse may be related to a scene of perdition in a tour of heaven, in which the punishments of the wicked are described, and often recorded in books.[170] Conjectural reconstructions of lines 2b–3a suggest either ⲡ.ⲭⲱⲱⲙⲉ ⲙ̄ⲡ[ⲱ]ⲛ̄ϩ ("the Book of Life")[171] or ⲡ.ⲭⲱⲱⲙⲉ ⲙ̄ⲡ[ⲟⲅⲱ]ⲛ̄ϩ ("the Book of the Revelation").

Fragment 20 Fragment 20 is a portion of a column with no margins visible on either side. 20H.2–6 concerns "every faithful woman," but it is unknown if this is an idealized woman, as in a parable,[172] or a woman character in the Gospel of the Savior, such as Mary Magdalene, who is not attested in this gospel (see comments on 12:6).

Fragment 20F.1–5 appears to be mostly the narrator's comments, which twice make reference to "the Savior," indicating the text is probably part of the Gospel of the Savior. The antecedent to the pronoun "he" (ϥ-; 20F.4) is apparently the Savior, but one of the apostles, or someone else (e.g., ⲁϥⲡⲱⲧ also in Mark 14:51–52), is described as having fled, suggesting a possible fulfillment of the predictions of the fleeing apostles in 4:3, 5, 7. This is followed by an opening address (line 6), apparently by the Savior to Judas, the betrayer (i.e., Judas Iscariot), or Jude, the brother of Jesus (also called Didymus and Thomas, i.e., the "Twin"). It is unclear whether this text is part of the expected betrayal and arrest scene of the Gospel of the Savior (cf. 4:2).

Fragment 21 Fragment 21 is a portion of a column with no margins visible on either side. 21F.3 has the word "shadow," which twice appears in the Gospel of the Savior (cf. 9:2; p. 122.31). 21H.2 has the word "world" ($\kappa\acute{o}\sigma\mu o s$), which occurs at least 15 times among the fragments.

Fragment 22 Fragment 22 is a central portion of a column with no margins visible on either side. 22H.1–6 has several words, but no extended syntax.

---

169 Cf. GkApocPaul 22–23,31 (Schneemelcher and Wilson, 2.726–730).
170. Cf. AscenIs 9:19–23; 1 Enoch 89:61–64; 98:8; Dan 7:10; Rev 3:5; 20:12.
171. Cf. Rev 3:5; 13:8; 17:8; ApocZeph 3:7.
172. Cf. Luke 15:8–9.

Fragment 22F.1–3 appears to make reference to the preaching of the apostles, possibly a commissioning scene,[173] but the relevance of this activity to the Gospel of the Savior is unclear. The scribe's period in line 5, followed by the Greek word for "or" ($\H{\eta}$) indicates the beginning of a new sense unit.

Fragment 23 Fragment 23 is a central portion of a column with no margins visible on either side. 23F.1–5 has several words, but no extended syntax, although the word "appear," suggests a visual revelation. The partial phrase "the] country ($\chi\acute{\omega}\rho\alpha$) of the[" is identical to Horner's Coptic edition of Matt 8:28, Mark 5:1, and Luke 8:26 (ⲧⲉⲭⲱⲣⲁ ⲚⲚ). But there the phrase is part of the opening of a miracle story, an exorcism, a popular genre not attested in extant fragments of GSav. 23H.1–6 has no extended syntax or significant lexical connections with the other fragments.

Fragment 24 Fragment 24 is a central portion of a column with no margins visible on either side. Fragment 24F.2–6 has no extended syntax or significant lexical connections with the other fragments, while 24H.2–6 appears to be a list, with the Greek word "liter," or "pound," ($\lambda\acute{\iota}\tau\rho\alpha$[174]) occurring four times in four lines. It is unclear whether the word is plural only in its third occurrence here. It is not possible to identify the text with either of the two occurrences of the word in the New Testament.[175] However, other neutral terms can find repeated use in a gospel text, suggesting that this text could be part of the Gospel of the Savior; note, for example, Luke 19:13–25, where the Greek word "mina," or "pound" ($\mu\nu\hat{\alpha}$), also a word concerning measurement, occurs nine times in 13 verses. The same phenomenon can occur in apocalyptic texts in which a visionary describes heavenly phenomena with terms that are repeated at length.[176]

Fragment 25 Fragment 25 is a central portion of a column with no margins visible on either side. 25F.4–5 has the word "kill" (cf. 14:13), and the resumptive phrase "now therefore," common in the Gospel of the Savior (see comments on 2:2). After another occurrence of the resumptive phrase, 25H.2 includes a partial address ("O my") possibly from the Son to the Father (cf. 14:14, 17, 23; p. 115.29), or the Savior to the apostles (cf. 6:2; 12:10; 9H.3b–5), but the rest of the text is too fragmentary for any useful comments.

Fragments (small) from center of a column

Fragments 26–27 No margins, a few words are visible.

Fragments (small) with no legible letters

Fragments 28–30 No legible letters.

---

173. Cf. Matt 28:19; Mark 16:15; Luke 24:47; Acts 1:8.
174. A Roman pound of 12 ounces (327.45 grams).
175. Cf. John 12:3; 19:39.
176. Cf. the word "days" in 2 Enoch 13:3; "gates" in 3 Enoch 8:1; "letters" in 13:1; 41:1–2.

Plates

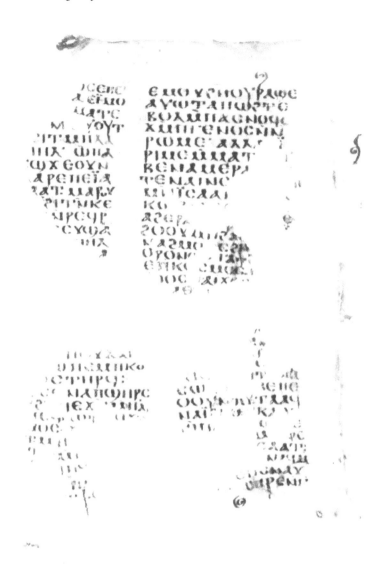

Foto: Margarete Busing   Jahr 1997

37   38   39   41   42   43   44   45   46   47   48   49   51

1H (A), p. 108

37   38   39   41   42   43   44   45   46   47   48   49   51

1H (B), p. [113]

Foto. Margarete Busing   Jahr 1997

2F (A), p. [106]

2

Foto: Margarete Busing   Jahr 1997

37   38   39   41   42   43   44   45   46   47   48   49   51

Foto: Margarete Busing   Jahr: 1997

2H (A), p. 100

Foto: Margarete Busing   Jahr 1997

2H (B), p. [105]

Foto: Margarete Busing   Jahr: 1997

3F, p. [98]

3H, p. [97]

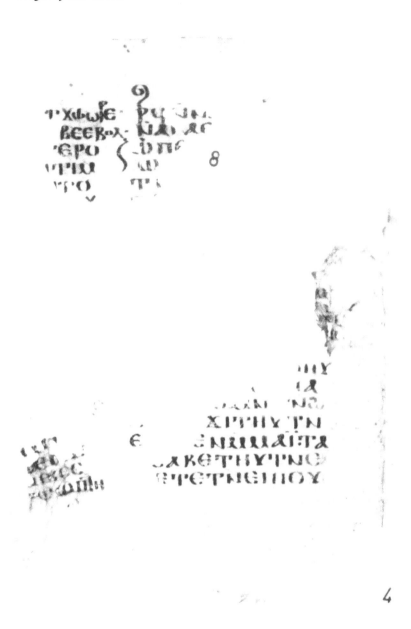

Foto: Margarete Busing   Jahr: 1997

4F (A), 122*

Foto: Margarete Busing   Jahr: 1997

4F (B), 115*

Foto: Margarete Busing   Jahr: 1997

37   38   39   41   42   43   44   45   46   47   48   49   51

4H (A), 116*

Foto: Margarete Busing   Jahr 1997

5

Foto: Margarete Büsing   Jahr: 1997

5H

6F

7

7F

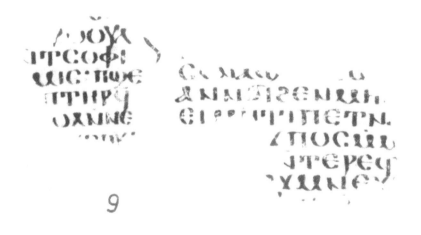

9

9F

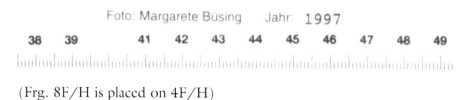

Foto: Margarete Büsing   Jahr: 1997

(Frg. 8F/H is placed on 4F/H)

6H

7H

9H

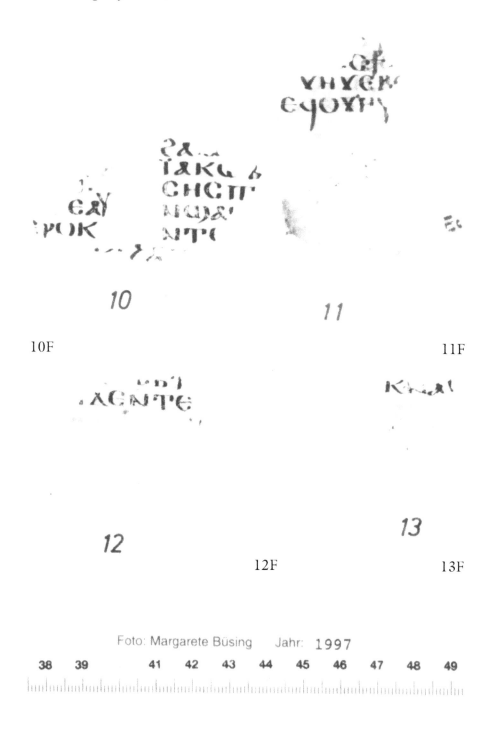

10

10F

11

11F

12

12F

13

13F

11H

10H

13H

12H

Foto: Margarete Busing   Jahr: 1997

38   39   41   42   43   44   45   46   47   48   49

14

14F

15

15F

14H

15H

16F   17F   18F

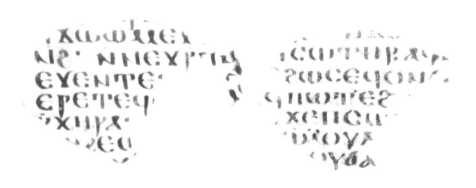

19F   20F

Foto: Margarete Büsing   Jahr: 1997

18H

17H 16H

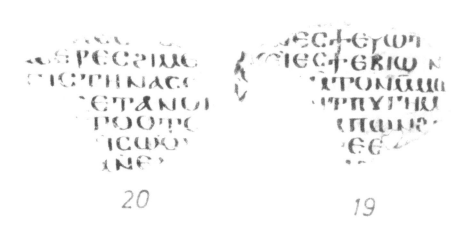

20

19

20H 19H

Foto: Margarete Büsing   Jahr: 1997

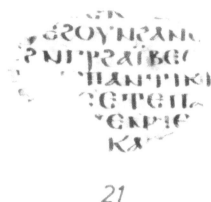

21

21F

22F

23

23F

24

24F

Foto: Margarete Büsing   Jahr: 1997

22

21H

22H

24H

23H

Foto: Margarete Büsing   Jahr: 1997

25   25F

26   26F

27   27F

28   28F

29   29F

30   30F

Foto: Margarete Büsing   Jahr: 1997

38   39   41   42   43   44   45   46   47   48   49

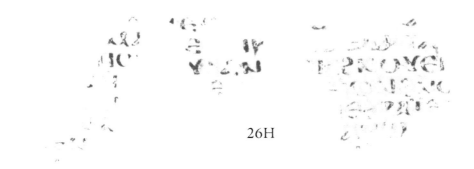

26H

27H

25H

30H

29H

28H

Foto: Margarete Büsing   Jahr: 1997

38   39   41   42   43   44   45   46   47   48   49

Indices

Coptic Words

ⲁⲙⲛ̄ⲧⲉ (m.) hades: p. 97.61
ⲁⲙⲁϩⲧⲉ (tr.) seize: frg. 14H.22
ⲁⲛⲁⲓ̈/ⲁⲛⲁ⸗ (intr.) be pleasing:
  ⲁⲛⲁϥ p. 99.10
ⲁⲡⲟⲧ (m.) cup: p. 114.8, 61
ⲁϣⲁⲓ̈ (intr.) to be numerous: frg. 5H.64
ⲃⲱⲕ (intr.) go: pp. 97.60; 107.32; 108.41;
  116.32
ⲃⲁⲗ (m.) eye: p. 100.36
ⲃⲟⲗ (m.) the outside/ⲉⲃⲟⲗ (adv.) out,
  outward, away:
    ⲉⲃⲟⲗ pp. 121.1; 122.2; frgs. 9F.6; 10H.3,
    37; 26F.3
    ⲉⲃⲟⲗ + ϩⲛ pp. 99.37; 113.1; frg. 22F.6
ⲃⲱⲗ (tr.) + ⲉⲃⲟⲗ to destroy, release: pp.
  100.48; 105.48
ⲉⲃⲓⲱ (m.) honey: frg. 19H.3
ⲉⲗⲟⲟⲗⲉ (m.) grape, vine: p. 97.30
ⲉⲣⲱⲧⲉ (m./f.) milk: frg. 19H.2
ⲉⲣⲏⲩ (m./f.) each other: p. 100.42
ⲉⲥⲏⲧ (m.) ground, bottom/ⲉⲡⲉⲥⲏⲧ (adv.)
  down, downwards: pp. 97.60; 113.31,
  39; frg. 23H.5
ⲉⲥⲟⲟⲩ (m.) sheep: p. 99.2
ⲉⲟⲟⲩ (m.) glory: pp. 107.16, 17, 18; 113.8;
  114.56; 121.32
ⲉⲓ̈ (intr.) come (cf. ⲛⲏⲩ): pp. 107.8, 13;
  113.31; frg. 25H.4
ⲉⲓⲛⲉ (tr.) take:
  ⲛ̄ⲧ⸗ p. 99.36
ⲉⲓⲣⲉ (tr.) to do: pp. 97.22; 98.29, 41, 45;
  99.10, 19, 35; 100.34, 45; 108.50, 62;
  113.6; 114.11; frgs. 5H.58; 19F.3, 6,
  7; 21F.3
  ⲉⲣ + ⲡⲙ̄ϩⲉ + ⲉⲃⲟⲗ become free: p. 108.52
  ⲟ (qual.) p. 107.27; frg. 20F.3
  ⲁⲣⲓ- (impv.) p. 108.29
ⲉⲓⲱⲧ (m.), ⲓ̈ⲱⲧ father: pp. 98.59, 61;
  99.11, 16; 107.33, 34; 113.41; 114.7,
  26, 59; 115.31; frgs. 17H.5; 19F.7
ⲕⲱ/ⲕⲁ-/ⲕⲁⲁ⸗ (tr.) to place, set, leave:
  ⲕⲱ- p. 99.5, 7, 14

ⲕⲁ- p. 107.22
ⲕⲁⲁ⸗ p. 98.57
ⲕⲟⲩⲓ̈ (m./f.) small thing, small amount (of
  time): p. 107.62; frg. 5F.23, 27, 30
ⲕⲁⲕⲉ (m.) darkness: p. 113.5
ⲕⲗⲟⲙ (m.) crown: p. 113.39
ⲕⲱⲛⲥ (intr.) pierce: p. 108.59
ⲕⲁϩ (m.) the earth: pp. 97.20; 114.58
ⲕⲱϩⲧ̄ (m.) fire: p. 107.42, 45
ⲙⲁ (m.) place: pp. 97.63; 98.48; 100.37;
  frg. 14H.26
ⲙⲉ (f.) truth: p. 108.63
ⲙⲉ (tr.) love: p. 99.16; ⲙⲉⲣⲓⲧ (m.; pl.
  ⲙⲉⲣⲁⲧⲉ) beloved: p. 114.39; frg.
  14F.30
ⲙⲟⲩ (intr.) to die: p. 114.33
ⲙⲟⲩⲕϩ̄ (intr.) to afflict, oppress: pp. 113.54;
  114.2
ⲙⲛ̄- (prefix before nouns or adjectives
  forming abstract substantives):
  pp. 97.9, 13, 17, 27; 108.64; 113.11;
  122.1, 3; frgs. 5F.22; 5H.61
ⲙⲛ̄ⲧⲣⲉ (m.) witness: p. 108.62, 64
ⲙⲟⲩⲣ (tr.) to bind: p. 97.62
ⲙⲁⲣⲉ-/ⲙⲁⲣⲉ⸗ (causative impv., conjugation
  base) let:
  ⲙⲁⲣⲟⲛ (absolute) p. 98.47
ⲙⲧⲟ (m.) presence:
  ⲙⲧⲟ + ⲉⲃⲟⲗ p. 100.39
ⲙⲁⲧⲉ (adv.) very much
  ⲉⲙⲁⲧⲉ greatly: p. 114.3
  ⲙ̄ⲙⲁⲧⲉ only: p. 114.38
ⲙⲏⲧⲉ (f.) midst: p. 107.59, 63
ⲙ̄ⲧⲟⲛ (m.) to rest (tr.): p. 108.58
  to rest (intr.): frg. 19H.4
ⲙⲁⲩⲁⲁ⸗ (adj.) alone: p. 98.57, 58
ⲙⲉⲉⲩⲉ (intr.) think: pp. 99.35; 100.47
  ⲣ̄ⲡⲙⲉⲉⲩⲉ frg. 19F.3
ⲙⲟⲟⲩ (m.) water: frg. 19H.6
ⲙⲟⲩⲟⲩⲧ (intr.) kill: p. 114.4; frg. 25F.4
ⲙⲏⲏϣⲉ (m.) multitude: frg. 9F.35
ⲙⲓϣⲉ (intr.) fight: p. 108.26

ⲙⲉϩ (prefix for ordinal numbers): pp.
106.16; 113.15; 114.63; 115.30
ⲙⲟⲩϩ/ⲙⲁϩ⸗ (tr.) to fill:
ⲙⲟⲩϩ frg. 5F.26
ⲙⲁϩ⸗ + ⲉⲃⲟⲗ: frgs. 5F.21; 5H.60
ⲛⲁⲁ-/ⲛⲁⲁ⸗ (nominal verb) to be great: p.
99.12
ⲛⲟⲃⲉ (m.) sin: p. 108.7
ⲛⲁⲓⲁⲧ⸗ (predicate exclamation) blessed
is/are: p. 97.15; frg. 9H.5
ⲛⲁⲛⲟⲩ-/ⲛⲁⲛⲟⲩ⸗ (nominal verb) to be good:
p. 99.4
ⲛⲟⲩⲧⲉ (m.) god, divine: pp. 99.19; 107.35,
36
ⲛ̄ⲧⲟϥ (adv.) but, rather (in contrasts): pp.
106.11; 107.31; 108.39, 44
ⲛⲁⲩ (tr.) to see: pp. 100.1, 49; 107.1, 3, 21,
29; 108.61; 113.13
ⲛⲏⲩ (qual. of ⲉⲓ, to come) be coming: frg.
23H.5
ⲛⲉϩⲡⲉ (intr.) to wail: p. 106.44
ⲛⲟⲩϫⲉ (tr.) to cast: p. 113.38
ⲟⲉⲓϣ (m.) a call, a cry/ⲧⲁϣⲉⲟⲉⲓϣ (tr.) to
proclaim: frg. 22F.3
ⲟⲛ (adv.) again, also: p. 97.59; 114.24; frg.
25H.4
ⲟϩⲉ (m.) (sheep-)fold: p. 99.2
ⲡⲉ (f.) heaven, sky:
ⲡⲉ (sg.) p. 113.16; 122.62; frg. 22H.5
(cf. ⲧⲡⲉ)
ⲡⲏⲩⲉ (pl.) pp. 97.14, 18; 100.40, 51;
113.1
ⲡⲏⲟⲩⲉ (pl.) p. 113.9
ⲡⲱⲱⲛⲉ (tr.) change: p. 107.17
ⲡⲱⲣϣ (tr.) spread: frg. 23H.6
ⲡⲁⲧ (f.) knee: p. 114.25
ⲡⲱⲧ (intr.) flee: p. 98.53, 56; 100.46;
113.26; frg. 20F.4
ⲡⲱϩ (intr.) attain: p. 113.15
ⲡⲱϩⲧ̄/ⲡⲁϩⲧ⸗ (tr.) pour, bend:
ⲡⲱϩⲧ̄ + ⲉⲃⲟⲗ: to pour out: p. 114.34
ⲡⲁϩⲧ⸗ p. 114.25
ⲡⲉϫⲉ-/ⲡⲉϫⲁ⸗ to say:
ⲡⲉϫⲁϥ pp. 97.32; 100.2; 107.11, 57, 61;
121.28; frgs. 9H.3; 14F.25; 14H.28
ⲡⲉϫⲁⲛ p. 107.4
ⲣⲟⲉⲓⲥ (intr.) to watch: p. 100.43
ⲣⲕⲣⲓⲕⲉ (f.) to slumber, to doze: p. 97.24
ⲣⲱⲕϩ̄ (intr.) to burn: p. 107.41
ⲣⲓⲙⲉ (intr.) to weep: p. 106.9, 43; 108.43;
113.54; 114.38
ⲣⲱⲙⲉ (m.) man, person: p. 98.31; 99.15,

19; 114.37
ⲡⲙ̄ⲙⲁⲟ (m.) rich man or person: frgs. 5F.20,
22; 5H.59, 61
ⲡⲙ̄ϩⲉ (m./f.) free man or person: p. 108.50,
52
ⲣ̄ⲣⲟ (m./f.) king/queen:
ⲣ̄ⲣⲟ p. 108.17, 19
ⲙⲛ̄ⲧⲉⲣⲟ p. 97.9, 13, 17, 27; 122.3
ⲣⲁⲧ⸗/ⲉⲣⲁⲧ⸗ (m.) foot, lowest part: p.
114.43
ⲣⲁϣⲉ (intr.) to rejoice: pp. 106.10, 42;
108.9, 15, 44 (m.) joy: p. 108.37
ϩⲛ̄ ⲟⲩ- (adverbial use): pp. 98.27, 30;
114.33
ⲣⲱϩⲧ (tr.) to strike: p. 98.64
ⲥⲁ (m.) side: p. 100.37
ⲥⲱⲃⲉ (intr.) to laugh: p. 106.41
ⲥⲱⲃⲧⲉ (qual.) ready:
ⲥⲃⲧⲱⲧ p. 114.32
ⲥⲙⲟⲩ (tr.) to bless:
ⲥⲙⲁⲙⲁⲁⲧ (qual.) p. 100.5
ⲥⲙⲓⲛⲉ (tr.) to establish:
ⲥⲙⲛ̄ⲧ⸗ frg. 9H.2
ⲥⲙⲟⲧ (m.) form, pattern: p. 107.7
ⲥⲓⲛⲉ (tr.) to pass by:
ⲥⲁⲁⲧ⸗ p. 114.9, 61
ⲥⲛⲁⲩ (adj.) two: p. 114.63
ⲥⲛ̄ⲧⲉ p. 106.16
ⲥⲛⲟϥ (m.) blood: pp. 97.29; 105.13;
114.35
ⲥⲟⲡ (m.) time, occasion: p. 115.31
ⲥⲉⲡ- p. 114.63
ⲥⲡⲓⲣ (m.) side, rib: p. 108.60
ⲥⲟⲟⲩⲛ̄ (tr.) to know: pp. 98.27; 106.11
ⲥⲟⲩⲱⲛ- frg. 23F.4
ⲥⲱⲟⲩϩ (tr.) to gather: p. 107.49
ⲥϩⲁⲓ (tr.) to write:
ⲥⲏϩ (qual.) p. 98.63
ⲥϩⲓⲙⲉ (f.) woman: frgs. 19F.5; 20H.2
ϯ/ⲧⲁⲁ⸗ (tr.) to give:
ϯ pp. 108.14; 113.11; 114.46; frgs.
19H.2, 3; 24H.2
ⲧⲁⲁϥ p. 114.57
ⲧⲁⲗⲟ (intr.) ascend, mount:
ⲧⲁⲗⲉ frg. 5H.62
ⲧⲁⲙⲟ (tr.) tell, inform:
ⲧⲁⲙⲟ⸗ p. 107.9
ⲧⲉⲛⲟⲩ (adv.) therefore, now (+ϭⲉ now
therefore, now then):
ⲧⲉⲛⲟⲩ p. 108.6, 43
+ϭⲉ pp. 97.63; 98.42; 107.49; frgs.
25F.5; 25H.2

ⲛ̄ⲧⲉⲓϩⲉ p. 113.59

ϩⲏ (f.) front, beginning/ϩⲏⲧ⸗ before, in the presence of:
ϩⲓⲑⲏ p. 113.40
ϩⲏⲧⲕ̄ p. 106.40
ϩⲏⲧⲥ p. 107.28

ϩⲏⲃⲉ (intr.) to mourn: p. 106.43

ϩⲱⲃ (m.) thing, work, event, deed: pp. 98.24, 30; 108.16

ϩⲃⲟⲩⲣ (f.) left side: p. 105.46

ϩⲁⲓ̈ⲃⲉⲥ (f.) shadow: pp. 105.44; 122.31; frg. 21F.3

ϩⲙⲟⲩ (m.) salt: p. 97.19

ϩⲙⲟⲟⲥ (intr.) to sit: p. 114.45; frg. 17H.4

ϩⲱⲛ (intr.) to approach, draw near/ϩⲏⲛ (qual.):
ϩⲱⲛ ⲉ- p. 100.40
ϩⲱⲛ ⲉϩⲟⲩⲛ pp. 98.49; 107.40
ϩⲏⲛ ⲉϩⲟⲩⲛ p. 107.43, 45

ϩⲓⲛⲏⲃ (intr.) to sleep: p. 97.23

ϩⲁⲡ (m.) judgement/ϯϩⲁⲡ to pass judgement:
ϩⲁⲡ p. 114.44
ϯϩⲁⲡ p. 114.46

ϩⲣⲁⲓ̈ (m.) upper part/ⲉϩⲣⲁⲓ (adv.) upward
ⲉϩⲣⲁⲓ̈ ⲛⲥⲁ- p. 100.41
ⲉϩⲣⲁⲓ̈ ϣⲁ- p. 107.32
ⲧⲱⲟⲩⲛ̄ ⲉϩⲣⲁⲓ frg. 5H.52
ⲉϩⲣⲁⲓ̈ ⲉϫⲱⲕ frg. 5H.62
ⲉϩⲣⲁⲓ̈ ⲉ- frg. 25H.5

ϩⲏⲧ (m.) heart, mind/ⲛ̄ϩⲏⲧ (compound; see ϩⲛ̄-/ⲛ̄ϩⲏⲧ⸗) in the heart of: pp. 113.55; 114.3

ϩⲟⲧⲉ (f.) fear/ⲣ̄ϩⲟⲧⲉ and ⲟ ⲛ̄ϩⲟⲧⲉ (qual.) (see ⲉⲓⲣⲉ):
ϩⲟⲧⲉ p. 107.23
ⲣ̄ϩⲟⲧⲉ p. 100.45; frg. 5H.58
ⲟ ⲛ̄ϩⲟⲧⲉ p. 107.27

ϩⲏⲩ (m.) profit, usefulness/ϯϩⲏⲩ to give profit: p. 108.14

ϩⲓⲟⲩⲉ/ϩⲓ- (tr.) to strike, cast, throw:
ϩⲓ- p. 105.44

ϩⲟⲟⲩ (m.) day: pp. 114.44; 122.60

ϫⲓ (tr.) to take, receive: pp. 97.24; 105.12; 113.42; 122.61

ϫⲱ (tr.) say, speak: pp. 108.36; 114.26; frg. 14H.25
ϫⲟⲟⲥ p. 114.48; frgs. 14F.23; 22H.6

ϫⲟⲉⲓⲥ (m.) Lord: (the Savior as ⲡϫ .) pp. 97.32; 107.5, 12
(God the Father as ⲡϫ .) pp. 106.12; 107.37, 38
ⲣ̄ϫⲟⲉⲓⲥ p. 98.45

ϫⲱⲕ (tr.) to complete, finish:
+ ⲉⲃⲟⲗ pp. 99.17; 116.30
ϫⲱⲕ (intr.) to be completed, finished: frg. 5F.25, 32
ϫⲱⲕ (tr./intr.?): p. 105.16

ϫⲱⲱⲙⲉ (m.) book: frg. 19F.2

ϫⲛⲟⲩ (intr.)/ϫⲛⲟⲩ⸗ to ask:
ϫⲛⲟⲩϥ frg. 14H.24

ϫⲣⲟ (intr.) to become strong/+ⲉ- to overcome: p. 108.45, 48

ϫⲉⲣⲟ (intr.) to blaze: p. 107.43

ϫⲱⲱⲣⲉ (tr.) to scatter, disperse:
+ⲉⲃⲟⲗ p. 99.1
ϫⲱⲱⲣⲉ (m.) scattering, dispersion/ⲧⲙⲛ̄ⲧ+ strength: p. 122.1

ϫⲓⲥⲉ (intr.) to be exalted/ϫⲟⲥⲉ (qual.):
ϫⲓⲥⲉ frg. 5H.55
ϫⲟⲥⲉ p. 121.32

ϫⲱⲧⲉ (tr.) to pierce, penetrate: p. 100.50

ϫⲟⲟⲩ/ϫⲉⲩ- to send:
ϫⲟⲟⲩ p. 108.30
ϫⲉⲩⲧⲏⲩⲧⲛ̄ p. 108.32

ϫⲱϩ (tr.) to touch: p. 107.31

ϭⲱ (intr.)/ϭⲉⲉⲧ (qual.) to remain: p. 98.58

ϭⲱⲗⲡ̄ (intr.) to reveal:
+ⲉⲃⲟⲗ pp. 98.26; 100.38

ϭⲟⲙ (f.) power pp. 98.29; 114.8, 60

ϭⲱϣⲧ (intr.) to look, glance:
+ⲉⲃⲟⲗ p. 106.40

ϭⲓϫ (f.) hand: frg. 18H.2

ϭⲱϫⲃ̄ (intr.)/ϭⲟϫⲃ̄ (qual.) be small: frg. 5F.26

Greek Words in Coptic

ⲡⲣⲟⲫⲏⲧⲏⲥ (m.; προφήτης) prophet: p. 121.28; frg. 9H.36

ⲡⲩⲗⲏ (f.; πύλη) gate: p. 100.43

ⲥⲕⲁⲛⲇⲁⲗⲓⲍⲉ (intr., σκανδαλίζειν) to be offended: p. 98.54

ⲥⲟⲫⲓⲁ (f.; σοφία) wisdom: frg. 9F.3

ⲥⲡⲉⲣⲙⲁ (m.; σπέρμα) seed, offspring: p. 100.4

ⲥⲧⲁⲩⲣⲟⲥ (scribal abbreviation ⲥⲣⲟⲥ ; m.; σταυρός) cross: pp. 105.42, 47; 106.46; 122.35, 54; frgs. 5F.23, 28, 31; 5H.53, 57, 63; 7F.3; 7H.36; 11F.30; 11H.30

ⲥⲧⲟⲗⲏ (f.; στολή) robe: p. 113.43

ⲥⲱⲙⲁ (m.; σῶμα) body: pp. 98.44; 100.35; 105.12; 107.8

ⲥⲱⲧⲏⲣ (m.; σωτήρ) savior: pp. 100.1, 50; 107.24, 54; 113.14; frgs. 14F.24; 20F.2, 5

ⲧⲟⲧⲉ (adv.; τότε) then: p. 113.2

ϩⲩⲗⲏ (f.; ὕλη) matter:
ⲧ+ϩⲩⲗⲏ as ⲑⲩⲗⲏ p. 98.45

ϩⲩⲙⲛⲉⲩⲉ (tr./intr.; ὑμνεύειν) to sing: frg. 9F.39

ⲭⲉⲣⲟⲩⲃⲓⲙ (m. pl.; χερουβίμ) cherubim: p. 113.27

ⲭⲏⲣⲁ (f.; χήρα) widow: frg. 19F.6

ⲭⲱⲣⲁ (f.; χώρα) country: frg. 23F.5

ⲯⲩⲭⲏ (f.; ψυχή) life, soul: p. 99.5, 8, 14
ⲯⲩⲭⲟⲟⲩⲉ (pl.) pp. 97.61

ⲱ (vocative; ὦ) O:
+ⲓⲟⲩⲇⲁⲥ frg. 20F.6
+ⲛⲁⲙⲉⲗⲟⲥ ⲉⲧⲟⲩⲁⲁⲃ pp. 100.3; 107.50; frg. 9H.4
+ⲡⲁⲓⲱⲧ pp. 114.6, 27, 59; 115.31
+ⲡⲁ[? frg. 25H.2
+ⲡⲉⲥⲣⲟⲥ pp. 106.45; 122.35; frgs. 5F.23, 27, 30; 5H.53, 57, 63; 11F.30
+ⲡⲧⲏⲣϥ p. 122.32
+ⲣⲱ[? p. 108.34 +[? p. 106.9

ⲱⲥ (as ϩⲱⲥ; conjunctive; ὡς) as, that, indeed: p. 108.40; frg. 20F.3

ⲱⲥⲧⲉ (as ϩⲱⲥⲧⲉ; conjunctive; ὥστε) so that: p. 113.56

Proper Names

ⲁⲃⲣⲁϩⲁⲙ Abraham: p. 114.40

ⲁⲛⲇⲣⲉⲁⲥ Andrew: p. 97.31

ⲓⲁⲕⲱⲃ Jacob: p. 114.41; frg. 10F.34

ϩⲓⲉⲣⲟⲩⲥⲁⲗⲏⲙ Jerusalem: (ⲑⲓⲗⲏⲙ, abbr.) frg. 14F.27

ⲓⲟⲩⲇⲁⲥ Judas: frg. 20F.6

ⲓⲥⲁⲁⲕ Isaac: p. 114.41

ⲓⲥⲣⲁⲏⲗ (ⲓⲏⲗ, abbr.) Israel: p. 114.6, 13

ⲓⲱϩⲁⲛⲛⲏⲥ John: p. 107.10

Ancient Texts and Authors

Old Testament (Roman)

Genesis
1:4b 98n54
1:26 101n68
49:11 29
49:11b 90

Exodus
3:8 73
16:10b 101n67
24:9–18 96n33
24:17 101n67
28 107
33:18–34:8 (LXX) 101n68
37:19 (LXX) 113n148
38:21 113n148
40:38 101n67

Leviticus
9:23–24 101n67

Deuteronomy
32:14 29
32:14b 90n6

1 Kings
1:36 103n84
1:36 (LXX) 103n84
8:10–11 101n67
22:19–23 109n124
22:19 108n115

Psalms
62(63):1 (LXX) 13
68:18 91n8
107:14 91n8
109:9–15 120

22

21H

22H

24H

23H

Foto: Margarete Büsing   Jahr: 1997

38   39   41   42   43   44   45   46   47   48   49